BANFF
the STORY & the SIGHTS

Irving Weisdorf & Co. Ltd.
TORONTO • ONTARIO • CANADA

THE DISCOVERY

THE RAILWAY CONSTRUCTION job had been long and difficult. But now, in the fall of 1883, the Canadian Pacific Railway had broken the backbone of the mountains. The opportunity to look for that elusive metal—gold—had finally arrived for three young railway workers.

Frank McCabe and Tom and Bill McCardell set out on yet another prospecting trip. This time, they selected a rather insignificant looking mountain with some hopeful geological signs. After rafting across the Bow River, the men disembarked near one of the many streams flowing into the river. This one, however, was quite different. The water was warm.

The curious men followed the stream to its source—a small basin of sulphur water choked with logs. And just a short distance away, the foul, rotten-egg odour of sulphur rose from an ominous opening in the ground. After much discussion and with great trepidation, one of the three descended through the opening. The flames of the torch lit up a small cave which held clusters of stalactites like "great gleaming jewels" and a small, warm, emerald green pool.

The young men had found a gold mine of a very different sort. The financial advantages of the discovery were immediately apparent. The Cave and Basin Springs would not only soothe the tired muscles of railway workers—for a price—but would attract people with ailments from all over the world in search of the cure that the sulphur waters were purported to provide.

Unfortunately, the lucky prospectors were poor businessmen. It required only a few mistakes in trying to obtain ownership before word of the

First shack at the site of the springs, built by McCabe and the McCardell brothers, 1883.

discovery was common knowledge. The smell of money, it appeared, was as strong as the smell of sulphur in the springs. Soon a confusing array of claims and counterclaims landed upon the desk of the Superintendent of Mines.

His recommendation was clear: create a public reserve around the springs. It was a suggestion warmly received by Ottawa, for the government found in this proposal a partial cure to its own problems. In order to ensure the survival of a young nation called Canada, the government had been forced to undertake one of the largest engineering projects in the history of this nation—the construction of a national railway through some of the most difficult terrain in the world. The cost of construction had proven to be a major financial drain. The economy was very shaky.

The Cave and Basin, however, was an opportunity to help support the new railway and ease the pressures upon the thin strands of Confederation. By developing tourist resorts in the western mountains, the railway could be assured of ongoing revenues. As Sir John A. MacDonald succinctly put it, "These springs will recuperate the patient and recoup the treasury."

The Basin swimming area, ca. 1890.

BUILDING A PARK

AFTER MCCABE AND the McCardells received some financial compensation, the government set aside 25 square kilometres around the springs on November 25, 1885. Expanded and renamed Rocky Mountains Park two years later, Canada's first national park had a very clear function—it was to earn money. It was to be a cooperative business enterprise centred around the development of a unique resort and sanitarium catering to railway patrons.

The government, in close cooperation with the C.P.R., immediately set about to "build" a park. Modelled after contemporary European and American parks, the new park was to be tidy, attractive, and entertaining. This meant the construction of opulent hotels and restaurants, the development of hot springs spas, the careful planting and tending of gardens, and the development of major recreational facilities.

The construction was successful. Rocky Mountains Park became one of Canada's best-known tourist resort areas. It was most definitely not a wilderness preserve. Indeed, this concept was entirely inconsistent with the realities of the day. Wilderness was more than abundant and was certainly in no need of protection. Income generation, not wilderness preservation, was to be the goal.

Banff Avenue, 1887.

It was the dream of the vice-president of the C.P.R. —William Van Horne—to provide deluxe accommodation in some of the most spectacular areas of the Rocky Mountains. The original Banff Springs Hotel, completed in 1888, was made of wood and was the largest hotel in the world at the time. The buildings were subsequently faced with stone taken from Mount Rundle.

Banff Avenue looking towards Cascade Mountain ca. late 1880s.

The opening celebrations of the Grand View Villa. Note the sign on the horse blanket proclaiming "Hot Springs Grand View Bus Line," and the sign on the building advertising "ice cold temperance drinks." Ca. late 1800s.

Banff was recognized internationally as a recreational paradise
and Tom Wilson's pack trains were an indispensible means of
getting visitors into the back country.

Members of an expedition in camp near Waterford Lake, 1902. Prof. J. Norman Collie (with binoculars) discovered the Columbia Icefield.

Catch of 35 fish at Lake Minnewanka, ca. 1893.

THE CONSERVATION MOVEMENT

DURING THE FIRST decade of the twentieth century, a new philosophy began to make its presence felt—conservation. Conservation, in reality, was two competing movements. For some, the concept involved the preservation of wilderness for its intrinsic, intangible values. For most, however, conservation involved the setting aside of vast tracts of land for controlled resource exploitation that ensured the greatest possible returns over the greatest period of time.

It was this latter concept that prevailed. With the dramatic expansion of park boundaries, there was a major increase in the types of activities within those boundaries. Rocky Mountains Park was no longer just a tourist resort. It had now become the home of

resource-based industries and projects including large-scale coal mining operations, hydroelectric developments, and extensive logging operations.

Government officials saw no conflict. Indeed, the superintendent's annual report of 1904 stated that "the new mining village of Bankhead, instead of being a detriment to the beauty of the Park will, on the contrary, add to its many and varied attractions." Though parks had grown larger, the concept that they should pay their way continued as a pillar of park philosophy. The concept of wilderness preservation was a distant notion.

This was most apparent in the attitudes concerning wildlife. The Victorian concept of nature as being either good or evil did not permit the

Storage dam at outlet of Lake Minnewanka, ca. 1912—15.

Coal mines at Bankhead, ca. 1912. Bankhead was once a thriving mining town of 900 people. Established in 1903, the mine employed 275 men below ground and 195 above. The town was owned and operated by the C.P.R. and was noted for the very best in service. Poor quality coal and competition from mines in Canmore, Drumheller, and Lethbridge forced the closure of the Bankhead mines in 1922. The town disappeared soon after.

preservation ethic to extend beyond certain species. A park directive clearly illustrates this fact: "The Superintendent will let nature alone as much as possible...at the same time, he will endeavor to exterminate all those animals which prey upon others." Today this is not regarded as an ecologically sound policy, but ecology was a term which did not become prevalent until the mid-twentieth century.

The conservation movement did have one very distinct benefit. Park boundaries were greatly increased—so much so that Canada became the first country in the world to set up a specific agency to control park lands, the Dominion Parks Branch. The choice of the first commissioner was fortuitous.

A NEW DIRECTION

J. B. HARKIN HAD very distinct notions about national parks. From the first he believed that these lands should be used primarily for recreation and education in a wilderness setting, and that resource industries had no place in parks. Recognizing that established patterns of use did not change overnight, Harkin embarked upon a major public relations campaign to convince politicians and the public that a new direction was in order. His efforts were greatly aided by a new invention—the automobile.

The great hegemony of the railway had been broken. No longer were the western parks accessible only by means of rail, nor was the clientele limited to those of greater financial means. Parks were opening up to the entire population—and with greater industrialization in the cities, the natural beauty and relaxation of the wilderness was becoming more and more attractive.

Public attitudes began to change. As resource industries were gradually phased out, there was a much greater emphasis upon recreational facilities, such as golf courses, tennis courts, dance halls, formal gardens, swimming pools, ski facilities, and manicured beaches. Townsites were opened up and leases were issued to build homes and summer cottages.

The results of Harkin's work were ultimately enshrined in The National Parks Act of 1930:

> "The parks are hereby dedicated to the people of Canada for their benefit, enjoyment, and education...and such parks shall be made use of so as to leave them unimpaired for the enjoyment of future generations."

As part of this major realignment in philosophy, Rocky Mountains Park became Banff National Park.

The National Parks Act was an important step. Its policy stressed that resource exploitation was not to be permitted within National Parks. For the first time in history, the protection of lands for future generations was stressed as strongly as the benefit to the present generation.

The trend towards preservation as the underlying ethic of National Parks continues. Today we recognize that there are some 48 natural regions in

Banff Avenue, 1926.

Canada, and it is the goal of the Parks Branch to protect representative samples of each.

The development of a national parks philosophy has been a long and fascinating journey. Today Banff represents all phases of this evolution. The townsite, the swimming facilities, the ski hills, the golf course, the ruins of the Bankhead Coal Mines, and the hydroelectric developments at Lake Minnewanka all represent various stages in the evolution of the park concept.

Most important of all, Banff represents the preservation of one of the most dramatic landscapes in Canada and the world—the Rocky Mountains of the Canadian Cordillera.

This legacy must be treated with respect and infinite care...a wilderness heritage to pass on to future generations.

Raspberry Bay,
Lake Minnewanka,
ca. late 1800s.

No scene better symbolizes the mountain legacy protected by national parks than Lake Louise. The small cabin to the right in the above photo was the original Lake Louise Hotel.

Containing only two bedrooms, a kitchen, and a sitting room, the chalet was a far cry from the opulent chateau which replaced the small wood building.

THE MOUNTAIN LEGACY

THE ROCKY MOUNTAINS afford some of the most spectacular scenery to be found anywhere in the world. Within the 6,670 square kilometres of Banff's boundaries can be found two of the cordillera's mountain zones: the Front Ranges and the Main Ranges. Each zone has its own distinctive appearance and characteristics.

For over a billion years, sediments accumulated, layer upon layer, in a deep ocean basin. Scientists theorize that about 200 million years ago, as the volume of sediments increased, the earth began a process of major readjustment. The massive plates which comprise the surface of the earth began to change their direction of movement. The plate

containing North America, which had previously been moving east, reversed its direction and ploughed back into the sedimentary basin. So intense was the compression that blocks of sediments 12,000 to 15,000 metres thick were lifted, folded, faulted, and transported up to 200 kilometres from the original point of deposition in a process that moved from west to east.

The deepest and oldest part of the ocean depression—the first to be uplifted—became the Main Ranges. Because of thick deposits of sand and gravel, the sediments were only gently warped into large-scale upfolds and downfolds. Thus, the strata retain a generally horizontal position, giving the Main Ranges their "layer cake" appearance.

The shallower, newer part of the ocean basin did not have the deposits of sand and gravel and reacted quite differently to the stress of mountain building. These limestones and shales were severely disrupted. In some areas the rock layers were actually folded back on themselves. In other areas, the sheets of stone were lifted and pushed upon one another piggy-back style, like shingles on a roof. Thus, much of the Front Ranges are characterized by steep faces and sloping backs.

The process of mountain building was slow, with each pulse of movement limited to only a few centimetres per year. As each massive slice of sediments was forced upward, it was immediately challenged by the erosive power of water. The top layers of sediments were stripped away, exposing more ancient pages of earth's history. Since the Main Ranges were the first of Banff's mountains to be born, the erosive effect of water acted upon the rock mass for a longer period of time. These mountains thus reveal the oldest sections of Banff's story.

Rivers and streams born in the Main Ranges gradually dissected the rock sheets into the primitive precursors of today's mountains. One particular stream played an extraordinary role in the history of this country. That river was the early Bow River.

Virtually all other rivers in the area became trapped between the stone wedges. But the Bow River had sufficient strength to cut into the sheets of stone at the same pace the Front Ranges were rising. As a result the Bow River became one of the few passages into the mountains from the plains. It was this valley which was ultimately selected by the Canadian Pacific Railway in its bid to bind the nation of Canada from sea to sea. And it was the financial requirements of the railway and the discovery of a few rather insignificant looking springs which led to the creation of a new concept—national parks.

The rugged beauty of these mountains is a relatively recent experiment in terms of geological history. When water acts as the major erosive force, mountains tend to be more rounded. Rivers are abundant, lakes are not. Several million years ago, however, temperatures grew cold enough to permit the establishment of vast icefields along the continental divide. From these accumulation points, rivers of ice flowed into the valley corridors, the most important of which were the valleys of the Athabasca, North Saskatchewan, and the Bow systems.

The effect was dramatic. Water-carved, V-shaped valleys were widened and steepened into broad U-shapes. Valley walls were at times undermined with resultant rock slides. The freeze-thaw of the colder temperatures caused blocks of stone to be broken from the mountain front, thereby establishing the rough angular forms familiar today. Where ice was deepest and most active, massive basins were hewn from the bedrock cresting the spectacular valley lakes. On a smaller scale, ice which formed in depressions on mountainsides above the flow of the valley glaciers carved tiny alpine bowls called cirques. Several of these cirque glaciers would often chew at the same summit, resulting in turretlike, or pyramidal, mountain peaks.

(Facing page) Glaciers once covered the Canadian Cordillera, leaving only a few isolated peaks towering above a sea of ice. Today, glaciers remain in isolated pockets, the most notable being the Columbia Icefield.

LIFE IN BANFF

THE MOMENTS, THOUGH often fleeting, sparkle as vivid memories: the early morning mist rising from the still lake waters, the plunge of the osprey, the heart-stopping crash of wapiti through the forest, the delicate fragrance of an alpine meadow.

As with any nature experience, a true appreciation of the mountains cannot be rushed. You need patience and a willingness to relax your pace.

The diversity of the valley bottom allows the visitor the easiest opportunity to adjust to the slower pace. At elevations below 1,370 metres the environment is much drier. Only slight changes in soil drainage, sunshine, or wind are required to dramatically alter the ecological community. Abrupt shifts from dense stands of spruce and subalpine fir to pockets of grassland or open savannah forests of Douglas-fir are not uncommon. This mosaic of environments supports a wealth of quite different plants and animals in a very small area. As a result, one need not travel far or have undue patience to sight many of the residents of the valley.

The grasslands of the dry, south-facing slopes are characteristic of the valley bottom where larger animals, such as wapiti, sheep, and deer gather. These pockets of grassland are critical to their survival during the harsh winter season. Only here on these windswept slopes are snows sufficiently shallow to permit easy access to food supplies.

Somewhat less obvious are the smaller residents of the valley bottom. Colonies of Columbia ground squirrels which reside in the more open areas remain constantly on guard for coyotes and hawks, their chief enemies. Virtually all grassland residents have the dusty brown colour of their environment to avoid detection. In contrast, the saucy black and white magpie seems a little too obvious. However, there is a logic to this "clown's" appearance. The stark black and white coloration makes it virtually invisible in the light and shadow environment of the poplar forests where it often builds its nests.

Top to bottom: deer, Columbia ground squirrel, moose.

(Facing page) The valley floor is a rich mosaic of environments including deciduous forest, coniferous forest, grassland, and marshland.

19

Indian paintbrush.

Gray jay.

(Facing page) The subalpine is the largest ecological zone in the park, encompassing the extensive coniferous forests which cloak the mountain slopes. The subalpine is noted for a wide range of flowers, which creates spectacular natural gardens.

Greater patience is required in the subalpine. In the oldest spruce-fir forests the great interlocking branches steal most of the light from the forest floor. As a result, little ground vegetation is available for the larger animals, and only a few year-round residents call the mature forest their home. Skittish red squirrels, pine martens, and spruce grouse are seen rarely. Indeed, it is most often the alarm chatter of the squirrel which indicates its presence.

When fire has devastated a mature forest, however, a transitional lodgepole pine forest quickly takes its place. Living for only a few hundred years before the spruce and fir can reestablish itself, the lodgepole pine forest has a more open canopy which permits greater sunlight to reach the forest floor. The understory is much richer. In these transitional forests black bear, deer, sheep, and elk seek food and shelter during the summer months.

Two gray black birds break the rule concerning the need for stealth and patience. The gray jay and the Clark's nutcracker have a tendency to seek you out rather than vice versa. The unofficial name of the gray jay, "camp robber," indicates why these are often the most commonly sighted residents.

The alpine requires the most patience. In this cold, harsh environment all plant life must seek the safety of the ground to escape the drying winds and the cutting ice. In a treeless land, motion spells danger. As a result, most residents use camouflage and an ability to freeze at a moment's notice as their primary means of defence.

Rest quietly along an alpine trail and simply gaze over what at first appears to be an empty, barren, rocky meadow. Your patience will usually be rewarded. When the residents feel secure, motion resumes. What first appeared to be a pile of boulders suddenly becomes the focus of activity for the tiny pika, which gathers, cures, and stores cut vegetation as a form of hay, and the larger, lazier marmot, which relies on its fat deposits to support it through its winter hibernation. Even when moving, the master of camouflage, the ptarmigan, remains difficult to locate. Often you must rely on the soft

Mountain goat, hoary marmot, moss campion.

(Facing page) The alpine is the harshest of the mountain ecological zones, and most plants grow close to the ground to avoid the wind and cold.

clucking of the parent to locate this alpine grouse and its brood of fluffy chicks.

While the larger mammals such as the caribou, sheep, and wapiti are easily seen in the stark meadows, quiet and stealth remain important to prevent a hasty retreat by these animals into the next meadow.

If you see the master of the wilderness, however, leave immediately. The grizzly is both powerful and potentially dangerous when surprised.

THE SPRINGS

THOUGH SOMEWHAT insignificant to our eyes today, these springs were a "hot" property a hundred years ago. Hot mineral springs meant curative waters. Curative waters permitted the creation of resorts. Resorts spelled visitors and revenue for the Canadian Pacific Railway. And the survival of the railway meant the survival of a young country called Canada. In terms of this country's history these springs are not at all insignificant.

All the springs originate as surface waters which seep through fractures created during mountain building. The deeper the fissures, the warmer the waters become and the greater the capacity to dissolve a substantial quantity of minerals. When the waters reach an impermeable layer (estimated to be as deep as several thousand metres) they are forced to the surface through another series of channels. As the waters cool, the minerals are released and redeposited as the friable stone called tufa.

Each spring has its own characteristic flow volume, chemical composition, and temperature. It is common for the temperature to fluctuate throughout the year depending upon the volume of

The Cave and Basin swimming complex.

Although the Cave once had stalactites hanging from the ceiling and walls, early generations of souvenir hunters have gradually removed them, piece by piece.

water entering the system and the rate at which the water is recycled. On occasion the temperatures will drop significantly for a long period of time. When this occurs the rate of deposition of minerals is superseded by the gradual removal of the stone through erosion.

Such a cooling occurred in the Cave and Basin Springs. It was the gradual eating back of the minerals which resulted in the distinctive shapes of the basins which hold the mineral waters. Originally the only entrance into the Cave was through the small hole in the top of the dome. Early park visitors

were forced to descend to the pool by means of ladders until the present passage was blasted into the Cave in 1887.

Two swimming and soaking complexes are located at the Upper Hot Springs and at the Cave and Basin Springs. The latter facility, originally constructed in 1914, has been completely refurbished and redeveloped as part of the 1985 Parks Canada centennial celebrations. As part of this redevelopment, a replica of the original bath house has been constructed near the Basin springs.

THE TOWNSITE AREA

THERE HAVE BEEN numerous towns within the borders of Banff National Park. Bankhead was a coal mining village; Siding 29 was a railway support town. There was the resort village of Minnewanka, and the mining community of Silver City—a town that for a few brief years rivalled early Calgary in terms of growth.

Only one community remains. Beginning as a support centre for the spas and springs, Banff townsite was designed to provide the best of services and facilities for its visitors. By 1900 Banff boasted eight luxury hotels, a myriad of coach roads leading to the surrounding natural features, dozens of shops, and excellent recreational facilities. For much of its early history, Banff was recognized primarily as a summer resort. By 1910, however, the C. P. R. and the government were advertising Banff as a winter playground. As demand increased, the town improved its older facilities as exemplified by the construction of the Cave and Basin buildings and the expansion of the Banff Springs Hotel.

There were no restrictions on who could live in Banff, and as a result there was an explosion in the number of summer cottages. In 1933 the establishment of the Banff School of Fine Arts added a major cultural centre to this growing community.

The passage of the National Parks Act in 1930 demanded a limit to the growth of the town. As park philosophy changed, it became apparent that uncontrolled growth would compromise the preservation ethic of the Parks Act. Today Banff administrators must manage a tourist centre that

Upper terminal of the Gondolas at the summit of Sulphur Mountain.

attracts millions of people each year.

For a century Banff has sustained the tradition of offering opulence and luxury at the threshold of wilderness, and it continues to take great pride in presenting to the world an extraordinary array of natural wonders that ring the town like gems.

(Facing page) View of Banff townsite from Sulphur Mountain.

A small representative herd of bison remain in the Buffalo Paddock.

Hoodoos on Tunnel Mountain.

(Facing page) Banff Springs Hotel.

Mount Rundle seen from the air, and reflected in Vermilion Lake.

LAKE MINNEWANKA DRIVE

MINNEWANKA IS A Cree Indian name meaning "Lake of the Water Spirit." If such a spirit does exist this would be the appropriate location. Lake Minnewanka, at 19 kilometres in length, is the largest and deepest of Banff's glacial lakes. Nestled between the spectacular Palliser and Fairholme ranges, the lake offers a passage deep into the park's northern wilderness.

Beneath the icy waters of the lake rest the remains of the small resort village of Minnewanka that flourished around the turn of the century. It was abandoned when the decision was made in 1912 to dam the outflow of the lake to provide electricity for Banff. When more electricity was required after the demise of the coal mining community of Bankhead, a new powerhouse was constructed in 1924. Finally, in 1941, as part of the war effort, the dam was greatly expanded to provide even more electricity. As a result of these hydroelectric developments, the depth of the lake was increased some 23 metres.

Views of Lake Minnewanka.

BANKHEAD

Rocky Mountain bighorn sheep.

THE RUINS OF THE mining community of Bankhead are a reminder of the development philosophy of early park management. Originally established to provide a local source of coal from Cascade Mountain for the railway, the town grew rapidly after the opening of the mine in 1903.

Bankhead was the pride of the government and the C.P.R. Not only did the mines produce half a million tonnes of coal annually, and employ close to 500 men, the town itself had some of the most modern facilities available anywhere. There were two dairies, a butcher, baker, laundries, general stores, a church, school, and recreational facilities such as a skating rink and curling rink. Services included electricity, running water, and sewers.

Despite the high thermal quality, the coal was severely broken. The railway had to import pitch from Pennsylvania to compress the coal dust and fragments into briquettes. The high cost of production and a series of labour strikes spelled disaster for the town. On June 15, 1922, the mine was closed.

Silver City was a short-lived boom town dependent upon poor grade ores. Only a Parks Canada display now marks the site of the village.

(Facing page) Castle Mountain.

THE BOW VALLEY PARKWAY

TIRED OF THE FAST pace of the Trans-Canada Highway? The Bow Valley Parkway offers a relaxing alternative. The roadway has been completely redeveloped to provide numerous picnic sites, viewpoints, and interpretive displays for visitors wishing a leisurely passage between Banff and Lake Louise.

One of the more intriguing sites along the Parkway is located soon after you begin the journey from Banff. As the name implies there is indeed a "hole in the wall" of Mt. Cory. It is believed that this is part of an old underground cave system that has been exposed by glacial action.

This channel is representative of a number of cave systems which have been carved from the limestones of the Rocky Mountains. Percolating water, following cracks and fissures in the stone, joined with carbon dioxide to create a weak acid. This acid is the primary force behind the intricate networking of channels that honeycombs many of these mountains.

Perhaps the most distinctive of all the mountains between Banff and Lake Louise is Castle Mountain, located near Johnston Canyon.

According to native legend, this spectacular 2,862 metre mountain is the home of the chinook—the warm wind which sweeps out of the mountains and onto the plains in late winter. Chinooks are created from air masses which first rise rapidly over the mountains and lose most of their moisture. Then, as the air rapidly descends, it is warmed. The only obstruction in this valley, Castle Mountain forces valley winds to ascend very abruptly. The air is cooled quickly with elevation and clouds stream from the summit. The result is that Castle Mountain appears to be creating the chinook directly at its peak.

By its appearance Castle Mountain is appropriately named. Scientifically it is classified as a *castleate* mountain. As the softer layers of stone erode, the harder, more resistant layers are undermined. Massive rockfalls result, ensuring the maintenance of these steep mountain fronts.

Once a small town rested in the shadow of this great mountain. In 1881 a Stoney Indian showed prospector J. J. Healy a piece of iron ore rich in silver and copper. The news spread rapidly, and as soon as the railway entered the region in 1883, over a thousand men swarmed to the site.

Log cabins, stores, brickyards, a lime kiln, and four mines immediately sprang to life. The quality of the ore was poor, however. No silver was ever found and the copper, lead, and zinc deposits were uneconomical.

By 1885 Silver City was nothing more than a memory.

JOHNSTON CANYON

LET YOUR IMAGINATION roam. Try to envision a picture of these mountains that is quite different from today's reality. Imagine a scene of rounded water-washed mountains deeply dissected by very steep valleys with precipitous walls. Mountains seem to be packed more closely together and the valleys are narrower. Torrential rivers and streams abound; lakes are rare.

What you have imagined is the landscape that existed for most of the life of the Rocky Mountains. Prior to the glacial age, water was the most important force of erosion. During the ice ages, when the ice sheets advanced, then retreated, several times, valleys were widened and the mountains were made more rugged and angular.

The deep canyon walls, the churning cauldrons of water, and the mists of Johnston Canyon represent the resurgent power of water since the retreat of the glaciers approximately 10,000 years ago. Following weaknesses in the stone, Johnston Creek has cut rapidly into these limestone sediments. The scene before you is a reminder of what was once the greatest sculpting tool in these mountains—water.

Parks Canada has constructed a unique trail at Johnston Canyon. Pathways are bolted directly above the creek, offering a rare opportunity to intimately experience the explosive power of water. These pathways also allow you to search for a strange little resident of the mountain streams—a small, plump, gray bird with a penchant for bobbing up and down. The water ouzel, or dipper, as it is more commonly known, builds its nest of mosses directly on the canyon wall. So thoroughly adapted to these streams is the dipper that it uses its wings to swim underwater, as well as to fly.

Johnston Canyon is an excellent example of the erosive power of water. Initiated only 10,000 years ago, after the retreat of the glaciers from this valley, Johnston Creek has managed to chip, scour, dissolve, and abrade the bedrock to create this impressive chasm.

LAKE LOUISE

DURING THE EVENING hours of August 23, 1882, distant rumblings echoed through the valleys around a survey camp. Tom Wilson, a packer for the C.P.R., questioned the Stoney Indian guides and was told that the thunder quite regularly arose from the "Lake of Little Fishes." Curiosity compelled Wilson to explore the source of the noise. He was ill prepared for the scene which awaited him.

It was, as he stated later, the most beautiful vision he had encountered throughout his many mountain journeys. Eleven mountains cradled the peaceful calm of an emerald green jewel. Reflected in the icy waters of the lake were the sources of the lake's thunder—the vast glaciers which clung to the steep slopes of towering Mt. Victoria and Mt. Lefroy. Collapsing blocks of ice from these glaciers reverberated throughout the valley.

Wilson immediately reported his discovery to the C.P.R. Although a railway station called Laggan was built 6.5 kilometres distant in 1883, it was not until 1890 that the first modest wooden hotel facility was constructed at the lake. It had but two bedrooms, a kitchen, and a large sitting room. Fire destroyed the building two years later. Rebuilt in 1893 the structure was expanded in 1900 and again in 1913. Once again disaster struck. Fire claimed the Chalet

in 1924. The following year the Chateau of today was built.

Lake Louise was well known for its opportunities for climbing, hiking, canoeing, and horseback riding. Whereas Banff was known for opulence and elegance, Lake Louise seemed to provide a touch more freedom and exuberance for its guests. For example, the C.P.R., somewhat exasperated with a few of its patrons, finally had to install revolving doors to stop riders on horseback from entering the lobby.

It is highly recommended that visitors take the 6.5 kilometre Plain-of-Six-Glaciers Trail to gain a spectacular view of the Victoria glacier. It was this glacier which left the large wall of broken rock rubble that dams the lake. If you wish to obtain a more overall picture of the area, the Lake Louise gondolas, situated across the valley, will take you to the 2,043-metre summit of Mt. Whitehorn.

Though appearing deceptively small when viewed from the Chateau, Lake Louise is actually eight kilometres long and two and a half kilometres wide. This aerial view of the lake and Chateau Lake Louise shows clearly the impressive size of the glacial lake.

MORAINE LAKE—
VALLEY OF THE TEN PEAKS

Moraine Lake has many moods. It takes only minor changes in weather or sunlight to alter the colour of the lake and the atmosphere of the valley.

IF ANY SCENE CAN challenge the beauty of Lake Louise it is Moraine Lake in the Valley of the Ten Peaks. Fed by the Wenkchemna (an Indian word for ten) Glacier, Moraine Lake appears at first as simply a smaller version of Lake Louise.

In contrast to the tranquil serenity which pervades the scene at Lake Louise, however, the close proximity of the ten towering mountain sentinels adds a fierce ruggedness to the picture at Moraine Lake. The mountains seem less hospitable, and there is a sense of the awesome powers involved in the creation of this landscape.

These are the Main Ranges. The mountains of this zone are characterized by relatively flat-lying sediments, in contrast to the steeply inclined layers in the Front Ranges near Banff. The lower reddish brown base to these mountains is the compressed sand and gravel of an ancient range of mountains that once stood in northern Canada over a billion years ago. They were dismantled and redistributed in the ocean basin as the layers called *gog quartzites*.

Around 600 million years ago, calcium carbonate, produced by sea life, became the major form of sediment. Compressed into limestone these deposits constitute the grayish upper half of the Main Ranges.

Moraine Lake does differ from Lake Louise in one major way. Whereas Lake Louise is dammed by a glacial moraine, Moraine Lake is blocked by the remains of two major rockfalls from the 2,314-meter Tower of Babel.

THE ICEFIELD PARKWAY

FROM RIVER VALLEY to alpine summit, the Icefield Parkway offers views so spectacular and so commanding that this roadway has been classified as one of the most beautiful scenic routes in the world. Do not rush this trip. Take time for exploration. You will be rewarded for your efforts.

Throughout your journey you will be flanked by an unbroken but constantly changing chain of mountains. From Lake Louise you remain within the Main Ranges. As you enter the Parkway from the Trans-Canada Highway you pass the oldest stone known in this area—layers of compressed sands and gravels that were deposited over a billion years ago. The closer you get to the Columbia Icefield, the younger the rock becomes in terms of geological age. These are the limestones which were deposited during the age of massive coral reefs which thrived in shallow sea waters. As your journey continues to Jasper you drop once again through time.

As you progress along the Parkway, particularly in the vicinity of the Bow Summit, look to the strata, or rock layers, in the mountains on each side of the valley. Notice how the rock layers dip at an angle. In your mind's eye, trace the layers from one side of the valley to the other. This massive dome you have created provides a graphic illustration of an anticline and the broad-scale upfolding of rock strata which occurs during mountain building.

During the gentle "warping" of the rock, the top of the anticline was strained and cracked to a greater degree than the rock at the edges of the dome. It was along these lines of weakness that erosion was most effective, carving a valley from the broken crest of this extraordinary wedge of stone.

Vast rivers of ice once filled this valley. Their action and movement created the broad, gentle U-shape that is visible today. Glacial fields remain localized in the valleys to the south where colder, moister climatic conditions offer safe havens.

On occasion very localized climatic conditions permit smaller glaciers to survive far from the icefields. Such is the case with the spectacular

The Icefield Parkway, showing the mountain strata.

Crowfoot Glacier.

43

Crowfoot glacier. This is a cliff glacier. The bench of stone upon which the majority of the glacier rests is fairly resistant to erosion. The strata directly above it, however, is less resistant. The ice continues to scour and pluck at this weaker strata, thereby increasing the size of its own little haven on the precipitous cliffs.

Glaciers are very sensitive to minute changes in climate. When the Crowfoot glacier was first named it had three very distinct branches. Because of a slight change in climate in recent decades the lowest of the claws has disappeared. The other two

Tons of pulverized stone known as "glacial flour" are released into the lakes by the glacial meltwaters. This produces the spectacular colours of the lakes of the Parkway. The best-known example is Peyto Lake (below), named after the mountain guide Bill Peyto, who explored the region in 1894.

branches remain healthy.

Of all the remarkable sights along the Parkway, none is more breathtaking than the extraordinary iridescent colours of the glacial lakes. The solution to the mystery of what creates these magnificent shades of turquoise rests with the glaciers that supply the lake water. As glaciers move they grind bedrock into fine powder known as glacial flour. Carried by meltwater streams to the lakes, this material is so fine that much remains suspended in solution. It is the reaction of sunlight to the fine particles which creates the colours of the lakes.

One need only think of a rainbow to remember that sunlight is actually composed of a myriad of wavelengths that we see as colours. When sunlight enters water without any particles, the red, orange, and yellow wavelengths are rapidly absorbed by the

surface waters. Greens are absorbed at a little more depth, leaving only blue to be reflected back to our eyes.

In glacial lakes something a little different occurs. The reds, oranges, and yellows are again quickly absorbed at the surface. The glacial flour in turn rapidly absorbs the blue wavelengths. As a result, only the green remains as the primary colour that is sent back to us.

Where streams flow into the lake the amount of sediment is so great and so close to the surface that occasionally the surface water does not even absorb the yellow wavelength. As a result, yellow green splashes of colour often play across these turquoise pools.

Waterfowl Lake.

(Below) Lake Louise.

COLUMBIA ICEFIELD

IT IS THE CROWNING glory of the Parkway:
a 385-square kilometre cap of glacial ice nestled in
some of the highest mountains of the Rockies. The
high elevation keeps temperatures sufficiently cold
and captures enough moisture to sustain the
Columbia Icefield and its tributary glaciers.

The largest icefield in the Rockies is also the
birthplace of three of Canada's major river systems.
The Athabasca River joins the Mackenzie to flow to
the Arctic Ocean; the Saskatchewan River flows
across the plains to Lake Winnipeg and then to
Hudson's Bay; and the Columbia River flows
through British Columbia and the United States to
the Pacific Ocean.

The most accessible of the glaciers is the
Athabasca. Snowmobile tours allow visitors access to
this 7-kilometre-long, 305-metre-thick river of ice.

Athabasca Glacier.

Unless accompanied by trained personnel, you should not approach a glacier. The ice moves constantly and poses many dangers, including crevasses up to 60 metres deep, drainage tunnels, called millwells, which lead from the surface of the glacier deep into its interior, and ice caves and ice blocks which can collapse without warning.

Technically, the Athabasca glacier is in Jasper National Park. To see Banff's most famous representative you must hike the trail called Parker's Ridge. The switchbacks lead past old fossilized coral reefs and exquisite alpine gardens. Once at the summit you are treated to an aerial view of the 11-kilometre-long Saskatchewan glacier. Parker's Ridge is also one of the few locations close to a resident population of mountain goat.

Copyright © 1986 by Whitecap Books Ltd.
Revised Edition 1990
Canadian Cataloguing in Publication Data

Bondar, Barry
  Banff chronicles

  ISBN 0-921978-14-6
  1. Banff Region (Alta.) - History. 2.
Banff Region (Alta.) - Description and
travel - Guide-books. 3. Banff Region
(Alta.) - Description and travel - Views.
I. Title.
FC3695.B5B65 1986 917.123'3 C86-091229-9
F1079.B5B65 1986

Typeset by The Typeworks, Vancouver, B.C.

Printed by D. W. Friesen & Sons, Altona, Manitoba, Canada

Published by Irving Weisdorf & Co. Ltd.
2801 John Street, Markham, Ontario, L3R 1B4

Photo Credits

Front cover: Larry Fisher, The Postcard Factory
Back cover: Glenbow Archives, NA-2755-6
pp.2—14: Glenbow Archives
    p.2: NA-637-6; p.3: NA-1097-4; p.4: NA-531-2; p.5:
    bottom: NA-2126-19, top: NA-4465-43; p.6: NA-
    2977-37; p.7: NA-529-23; p.8: NA-345-2; p.9: top:
    NA-3551-73, bottom: NA-237-38; p.10: NA-3544-22;
    p.11: NA-612-1; p.12/13: NA-554-2; p.13: NA-2977-
    14; p.14 top: NA-2977-17, bottom: NA-2977-27.

pp.15: Barry Bondar; p.17: Bob Herger, Photo/Graphics; p.18:
Travel Alberta; p.19 top and bottom: Terry Willis; p.19 middle:
Derek and Jane Abson, Photo/Graphics; p.20: Bob Herger,
Photo/Graphics; p.21 top right and bottom: Roger Laurilla,
Photo/Graphics; p.21 top left: Gunter Marx, Photo/Graphics; p.22
left: Roger Laurilla, Photo/Graphics; p.22 bottom: Derek and Jane
Abson, Photo/Graphics; p.22 top right: Barry Bondar; p.23: Fred
Chapman, Photo/Graphics; p.24/25: Roger Laurilla,
Photo/Graphics; p.26: Gunter Marx, Photo/Graphics; p.27,28 top:
Travel Alberta; p.28 bottom left: Roger Laurilla, Photo/Graphics,
bottom right: John Burridge, Photo/Graphics; pp.29,30 bottom:
Derek and Jane Abson, Photo/Graphics; p.30 top: John Burridge,
Photo/Graphics; p.31, John Burridge, Photo/Graphics; p.32 top:
Barry Bondar; p.32 bottom: Gunter Marx, Photo/Graphics; p.33 top:
Terry Willis, Photo/Graphics; p.33 bottom: John Burridge,
Photo/Graphics; p.34: Glenbow Museum, NA-160-1; p.35: Gunter
Marx, Photo/Graphics; pp.36,37: Travel Alberta; p.38: Bob Herger,
Photo/Graphics; p.39: Michael Burch; p.40: Bob Herger,
Photo/Graphics; p.41: John Burridge, Photo/Graphics; p.42:
Gunter Marx, Photo/Graphics; p.43: Travel Alberta; p.44: Gunter
Marx, Photo/Graphics; p.45 top: Bob Herger, Photo/Graphics; p.45
bottom: Jurgen Vogt, Photo/Graphics; p.46 top: Roger Laurilla,
Photo/Graphics; p.46 bottom, p.47 top: Barry Bondar; p.47 bottom:
Travel Alberta; p.48 Barry Bondar.

TABLE OF CONTENTS

Canada 4-5
The Crown in Canada (I) 6-7
The Crown in Canada (II) 8-9
"O Canada" 10-11
"God Save The Queen" 12-13
Historical Flags 14-15
Historical Boundaries 16-17
Ontario 18-19
Quebec 20-21
Nova Scotia 22-23
New Brunswick 24-25
Manitoba 26-27
British Columbia 28-29
Prince Edward Island 30-31
Saskatchewan 32-33
Alberta 34-35
Newfoundland 36-37
Northwest Territories 38-39
Yukon 40-41

Classroom Activity Pages:
    Teaching Suggestions 42
    Symbols around us 43
    Canadian flags 44
    Armorial bearings 45
    Personal coat of arms 46
    Floral emblems 47
    Stamps of Canada 48
    Canadian coinage 49

"For Additional Information" 51-52

The Dominion of Canada Chart (insert)

Note: Centre-fold to be extracted for display and/or framing purposes.

CANADA

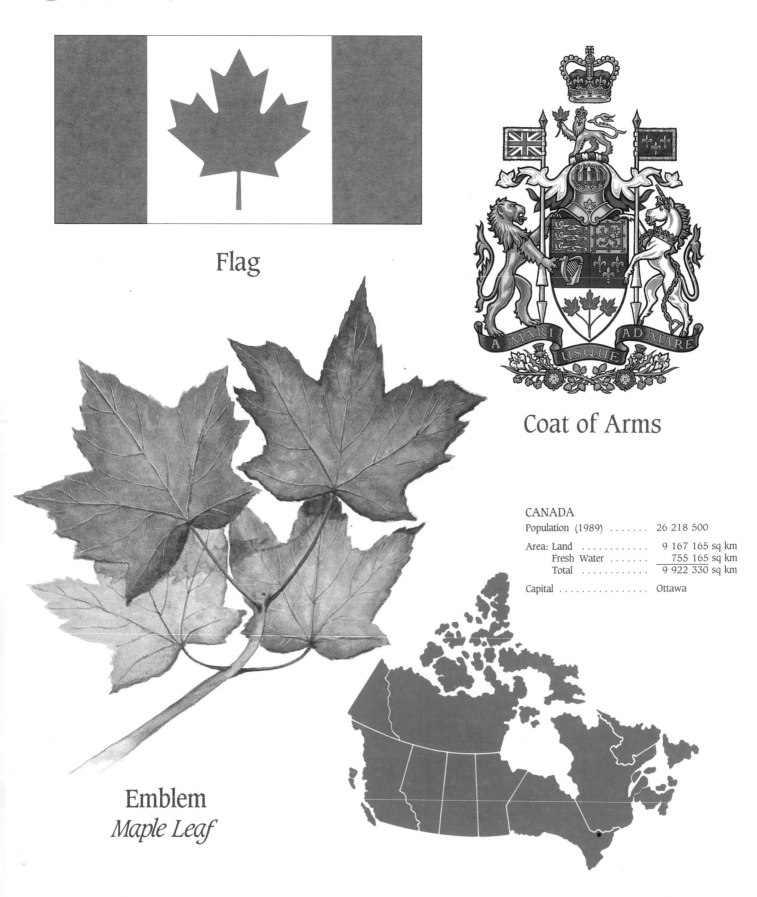

Flag

Coat of Arms

CANADA
Population (1989) 26 218 500

Area: Land . . . .   9 167 165 sq km
      Fresh Water . . . .   755 165 sq km
      Total . . . .   9 922 330 sq km

Capital . . . . Ottawa

Emblem
Maple Leaf

Origin of the name

In 1535, two Indian youths told Jacques Cartier about the route to "kanata." They were referring to the village of Stadacona; "kanata" was simply the Huron-Iroquois word for "village" or "settlement". But for want of another name, Cartier used "Canada" to refer not only to Stadacona (the site of present-day Quebec City), but also to the entire area subject to its chief, Donnacona. The name was soon applied to a much larger area: maps in 1547 designated everything north of the St. Lawrence River as "Canada".

Cartier also called the St. Lawrence River the "rivière de Canada," a name used until the early 1600s. By 1616, although the entire region was known as New France, the area along the great river of Canada and the Gulf of St. Lawrence was still called Canada.

Soon explorers and fur traders opened up territory to the west and to the south and the area depicted as "Canada" grew. In the early 1700s, the name referred to all lands in what is now the American mid-west and as far south as present-day Louisiana.

The first use of "Canada" as an official name came in 1791 when the Province of Quebec was divided into the colonies of Upper and Lower Canada. In 1841, the two Canadas were again united under one name, the Province of Canada. At the time of Confederation, the new country assumed the title — the Dominion of Canada. Taken from Psalm 72: "He shall have dominion also from sea to sea, and from the river unto the ends of the earth", the Fathers of Confederation chose the title wisely. They explained to Queen Victoria that it was "...intended to give dignity" to the union and that it was chosen "...as a tribute to the monarchical principle, which they earnestly desire to uphold." While the name of the country is Canada, its official title is the Dominion of Canada, reaffirmed by the *Constitution Act, 1982* that patriated the Canadian Constitution.

History

Ten provinces and two territories make up Canada today. However, in 1867 when the *British North America Act* was proclaimed creating the new Dominion of Canada, there were only four provinces — Ontario, Quebec, Nova Scotia and New Brunswick.

Three years after Confederation, Canada purchased Rupert's Land from the Hudson's Bay Company, which had been granted a charter to the area by the British government exactly two centuries before. Rupert's Land spanned all land drained by rivers flowing into Hudson Bay — roughly 40 percent of present-day Canada. This represented one-twentieth of all fertile prairie lands (almost 2.8 million ha), and the land around the company's trading posts — about 18,000 ha. The selling price was 300,000 pounds sterling.

Also, in 1870 Britain transferred the North-Western Territory to Canada. Previously the Hudson's Bay Company had an exclusive licence to trade in this area. When the Palliser and Hind expedition in the mid-1800s discovered that the prairies had enormous farming potential, the British refused to renew the company's licence. With the Hudson's Bay Company out of the area, Britain was free to turn it over to Canada.

The two newly-acquired regions, Rupert's Land and the North-Western Territory, were combined to form the Northwest Territories. *The Manitoba Act* of 1870 created the province of Manitoba from a small part of this area.

In 1871, the colony of British Columbia joined the union with the promise of a railway to link it with the rest of the country.

In 1873, Prince Edward Island, which had previously declined the offer to join Confederation, became the country's seventh province.

Yukon, which had been a district of the Northwest Territories since 1895, became a separate territory in 1898.

Meanwhile, Canada was opening up its west, just as its neighbour to the south had done before, and migrants from eastern Canada and immigrants from Europe began to fill the prairies, which were still part of the Northwest Territories. Then, in 1905, the provinces of Saskatchewan and Alberta were created completing the map of Western Canada.

The last addition to Canada came relatively recently. After great debate and two referenda, Newfoundlanders voted to join Confederation, creating the dominion's tenth province on March 31, 1949.

Armorial Bearings

Adopted:
By proclamation of King George V on November 21, 1921

Description:
The design reflects the importance of the four founding nations. The shield of the Royal Arms of Canada features the three royal lions of England, the royal lion of Scotland, the royal fleurs-de-lis of France and the royal Irish harp of Tara. On the bottom portion of the shield is a sprig of three Canadian maple leaves. The Coat of Arms is supported by the lion of England holding the Union Flag and the unicorn of Scotland carrying the flag of Royal France. The crest is a crowned lion holding a red maple leaf. At the base of the Royal Arms are the floral emblems of the four founding nations of Canada: the English rose, the Scottish thistle, the French fleur-de-lis and the Irish shamrock.

Motto

A MARI USQUE AD MARE
(from sea to sea)

Flag

Adopted:
By resolutions of Parliament on December 15, 1964 (House of Commons) and December 17, 1964 (Senate); proclaimed by Queen Elizabeth II to take effect on February 15, 1965, the day the maple leaf flag was first raised over Parliament Hill.

Description:
The flag is red and white, the official colours of Canada as appointed by King George V in 1921, with a stylized 11-point red maple leaf in its centre.

Previous flags included the Royal Union Flag (commonly known as the Union Jack), first flown over Canada in 1621, and the Canadian Red Ensign, a form of which was used from approximately 1870. The search for a new Canadian flag began in earnest in 1925 when a committee of the Privy Council began to investigate possible designs for a national flag. Later, in 1946, a select parliamentary committee was appointed with a similar mandate and examined more than 2,600 submissions. Then, and for the next 18 years, agreement could not be reached on a new design. However, as the centennial of Confederation approached, Parliament increased its efforts to choose a new flag. Our present flag was flown for the first time on February 15, 1965.

Proportion:
Two by length and one by width

CANADA

THE CROWN IN CANADA – I

The Queen's Personal
Canadian Flag

The Royal Cypher

The Crown

The
Governor General's
Flag

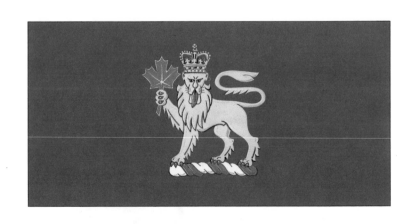

The Queen's Personal Canadian Flag

In 1962, Her Majesty The Queen adopted a personal flag specifically for use in Canada. The design comprises the Arms of Canada with The Queen's own device in the centre. The device — the initial 'E' surmounted by the St. Edward's Crown within a chaplet of roses — is gold on a blue background.

When The Queen is in Canada, this flag is flown, day and night, at any building in which She is in residence. Generally, the flag is also flown behind the saluting base when She conducts troop inspections, on all vehicles in which She travels, and on Her Majesty's Canadian ships (HMCS) when The Queen is aboard.

The Royal Cypher

The Royal Cypher is The Queen's monogram (Elizabeth II Regina) below a crown. It is used in insignia of Orders, in decorations and medals, on various badges, and on stationery. The use of the Royal Cypher denotes a close connection with the person of The Sovereign.

The Crown

Her Majesty Queen Elizabeth II, on Her accession to the Throne in 1952, decided to use a heraldic representation of the crown which closely resembles the St. Edward's Crown, used for the Coronation.

The Governor General's Flag

The coat of arms of the Governor General changes with each new Governor General, but the flag remains the same: the crest of the Royal Arms of Canada on a blue field. The crest consists of a lion wearing St. Edward's Crown, holding a red maple leaf in its front right paw, and standing on a wreath of red and white cloth. This flag was approved by Her Majesty The Queen in 1981.

The flag of the Governor General is flown, day and night, at any building in which His Excellency is in residence. Generally, the flag is also flown behind the saluting base when the Governor General conducts troop inspections and on all vehicles in which he travels.

THE CANADIAN CROWN

Introduction

Although Her Majesty Queen Elizabeth II is often referred to as Queen of the United Kingdom, it is not on this basis that Canadians offer Her allegiance. She is, quite separately, Sovereign of Canada by deliberate choice of Canadians. (She is similarly Queen of Australia, of Jamaica, of New Zealand, and of numerous other Commonwealth countries.) In fact, Canada has always been a monarchy — under the Kings of France in the 16th, 17th and 18th centuries, as colonies under the British Crown in the 18th and 19th centuries, and as a kingdom in her own right since 1867. The Dominion of Canada is, therefore, today the beneficiary of centuries of evolution from absolute monarchy, where the Sovereign actually ruled, to the modern constitutional monarchy, where the Sovereign reigns but does not rule.

At Confederation in 1867, the Fathers of Confederation specifically chose constitutional monarchy as part of the political framework of the new nation. The *British North America Act, 1867 (Constitution Act, 1867)* stipulated that "the Executive Government and authority of and over

Canada continues and is vested in The Queen." In 1952, Elizabeth II was proclaimed in Canada "by the Grace of God, of the United Kingdom, Canada and her other Realms and Territories Queen. . . . ." The most-recent reaffirmation of the monarchy in Canada is found in the *Constitution Act, 1982*, which repatriated our constitution from Britain. Any change to the position of The Queen or Her representatives in Canada, i.e. the Governor General and the Lieutenant Governors, now requires the unanimous consent of Parliament and the legislatures of all the provinces.

The Monarch Personifying the Nation

The Sovereign personifies the nation. She is, therefore, the personal symbol of allegiance, unity and authority for all Canadians, and the custodian of the democratic powers vested in The Crown. Conversely, the State is personified in The Sovereign in a constitutional monarchy. This explains one of the key characteristics of the Canadian system of government. Federal and provincial legislators, Cabinet Ministers, public servants, military and police personnel all swear allegiance to The Queen (not to a flag or constitution); so do new citizens at citizenship court ceremonies. Elections are called and laws are promulgated in The Queen's name.

The Canadian historian W.L. Morton points out that, because of this allegiance to a person uniting Canadians at the top, "there is no pressure for uniformity. . . Anyone. . .can be a subject of The Queen and a citizen of Canada without in any way ceasing to be himself." The monarchy is therefore well adapted to Canada's regional, bilingual, and multicultural character.

The Queen and the Governor General

As early as 1926 (with the Balfour Declaration), the Governor General ceased to represent the British government and became the personal representative of The Sovereign in Canada. This was confirmed by the *Statute of Westminster (1931)*. Powers of The King were gradually transferred to the Governor General, culminating with the Letters Patent of 1947, which authorized the Governor General to exercise all the powers of the Sovereign in right of Canada, on the advice of the Canadian government.

The Queen is the Canadian Head of State; the Governor General, as Her Majesty's personal representative, is accorded the honours and privileges usually given to a Head of State. Her Majesty's presence in Canada does not negate the powers of the Governor General.

CANADA

THE CROWN IN CANADA – II
The Flags of the Lieutenant Governors

Ontario

Quebec

Nova Scotia

New Brunswick

Manitoba

British Columbia

Prince Edward Island

Saskatchewan

Alberta

Newfoundland

The Flags of the Lieutenant Governors

At the request of individual provincial governments, the Governor General has approved, in the name of The Queen, new standards to be used by the Lieutenant Governors of Ontario, New Brunswick, Saskatchewan, Alberta, Prince Edward Island, British Columbia, Manitoba and Newfoundland. These standards identify them as The Queen's representatives at the provincial level. The new standard is a royal blue flag charged with the shield of the arms of the province surrounded by a circlet of 10 gold stylized maple leaves, representing the provinces of Canada. Above all of this is a St. Edward's crown, which symbolizes the dignity of the Lieutenant Governor as The Sovereign's representative in the province.

The new design was approved in 1981 for Ontario (June 27), New Brunswick (September 22), Saskatchewan (September 26), Alberta (September 26), and Prince Edward Island (November 18). British Columbia's design was approved on February 1, 1982, Manitoba's on May 11, 1984 and Newfoundland's on January 31, 1987.

Since 1952, the Lieutenant Governor of Quebec uses a blue flag charged with the Arms of Quebec within a white disk. Nova Scotia uses the flag as authorized by an order-in-council, dated August 7, 1869, and signed by Queen Victoria. It includes the Royal Union Flag, being charged with the shield of arms of the province within a white disk circled by a garland of green maple leaves.

The Collective Canadian Crown

An interesting characteristic of the Canadian Head of State, or the "Canadian Crown", is what has been called the "team of governors" or "collective headship of State". The Governor General and Lieutenant Governors together represent The Queen, embody The Crown in right of Canada and of the provinces respectively, and exercise The Queen's powers on Her behalf in their jurisdictions. The Canadian Crown benefits from the mystique and historic prestige of an ancient, hereditary monarchy, while making it thoroughly indigenous through the local representatives of The Sovereign. One cannot do without the other; the Governor General and Lieutenant Governors derive their legitimacy and prestige from The Queen. By virtue of Her Majesty's representatives in Canada, The Crown is truly a Canadian institution.

The Queen and The Lieutenant Governors

The relationship between The Sovereign and the Lieutenant Governors was not envisaged in the same way as it was with the Governor General when the Dominion of Canada was first formed by the *British North America Act* in 1867. Rather than being considered as The Queen's direct representatives in the provinces, the Lieutenant Governors were seen as the Governor General's representatives and agents of the federal government, which continues to be responsible for their appointment and payment. However, custom, evolution, convention and legal precedents have fundamentally altered the perspective of that office. The Lieutenant Governors, though continuing to be federal appointees and holding some residual federal powers, are seen as The Queen's direct and personal representatives, embodying The Crown in right of the provinces.

Therefore, the Lieutenant Governors act with respect to the provinces as the Governor General does to Canada and exercise The Queen's powers as Head of State at the provincial level. The Lieutenant Governors and the Provincial Crown, which they personify, symbolize the sovereignty of the provincial governments within the federation.

CANADA

O CANADA

O Canada!
   Our home and native land!
True patriot love
   in all thy sons command.
With glowing hearts
   we see thee rise,
The True North
   strong and free!
From far and wide,
   O Canada,
We stand on guard
   for thee.
God keep our land
   glorious and free!
O Canada,
   we stand on guard for thee.
O Canada,
   we stand on guard for thee.

O Canada!
   Terre de nos aïeux,
Ton front est ceint
   de fleurons glorieux!
Car ton bras
   sait porter l'épée,
Il sait porter
   la croix!
Ton histoire
   est une épopée
Des plus
   brillants exploits.
Et ta valeur,
   de foi trempée,
Protégera nos foyers
   et nos droits,
Protégera nos foyers
   et nos droits.

The
Maple Leaf

The Beaver

The National Anthem

"O Canada" was proclaimed Canada's national anthem on July 1, 1980, 100 years after it was first sung on June 24, 1880. The music was composed by Calixa Lavallée, a well-known composer; French lyrics to accompany the music were written by Sir Adolphe-Basile Routhier. The song gained steadily in popularity. Many English versions have appeared over the years. The version, on which the official English lyrics are based, was written in 1908 by Mr. Justice Robert Stanley Weir. The official English version includes changes recommended in 1968 by a Special Joint Committee of the Senate and House of Commons. The French lyrics remain unaltered.

OTHER CANADIAN SYMBOLS

The Maple Leaf

The maple leaf was first associated with Canada as early as the 1700s. In 1834, the first St. Jean Baptiste Society in North America made the maple leaf its emblem. In 1848, the Toronto literary annual *The Maple Leaf* referred to it as the chosen emblem of Canada. By 1860, the maple leaf was incorporated into the badge of the 100th Regiment (Royal Canadians) and was used extensively in decorations for the visit of The Prince of Wales that year.

Alexander Muir wrote *The Maple Leaf Forever* as Canada's confederation song in 1867; it was regarded as the national song for several decades. The coats of arms created the next year for Ontario and Quebec both included the maple leaf.

The maple leaf today appears on the penny. However, between 1876 and 1901, it appeared on all Canadian coins. The modern one-cent piece has two maple leaves on a common twig, a design that has gone almost unchanged since 1937.

During the First World War, the maple leaf was included in the badge of the Canadian Expeditionary Force. Since 1921, the Royal Arms of Canada have included three maple leaves as a distinctive Canadian emblem. With the proclamation of Canada's new flag in 1965, the maple leaf has become the most prominent Canadian symbol.

The Beaver

After the early European explorers had realized that Canada was not the spice-rich Orient, the main mercantile attraction was the beaver population numbering in the millions. In the late 1600s and early 1700s, the fashion of the day demanded fur hats, which needed beaver pelts. As these hats became more popular, the demand for the pelts grew.

King Henry IV of France saw the fur trade as an opportunity to acquire much-needed revenue and to establish a North American empire. Both English and French fur traders were soon selling beaver pelts in Europe at 20 times their original purchase price.

The trade of beaver pelts proved so lucrative that the Hudson's Bay Company honoured the buck-toothed little animal by putting it on the shield of its coat of arms in 1678. (Sir William Alexander, who was granted title to Nova Scotia in 1621, had been the first to include the beaver in a coat of arms.).

The Hudson's Bay Company shield consists of four beavers separated by a red St. George's Cross and reflects the importance of this industrious rodent to the company. A coin was created to equal the value of one beaver pelt.

Also, in 1678 Louis de Buade de Frontenac, then Governor of New France, suggested the beaver as a suitable emblem for the colony, and proposed it be included in the armorial bearings of the City of Quebec. In 1690, in commemoration of France's successful defence of Quebec, the "Kebeca Liberata Medal" was struck. A seated woman, representing France, with a beaver at her feet, representing Canada, appeared on the back.

The beaver was included in the armorial bearings of the City of Montreal when it was incorporated as a city in 1833. Sir Sandford Fleming assured the beaver a position as a national symbol when he featured it on the first Canadian postage stamp — the 'Three Penny Beaver' of 1851.

Despite all this recognition, the beaver was close to extinction by the mid-19th century. There were an estimated six million beaver in Canada before the start of the fur trade. During its peak, 100,000 pelts were being shipped to Europe each year; the Canadian beaver was in danger of being wiped out. Luckily, about that time, Europeans took a liking to silk hats and the demand for beaver pelts all but disappeared.

The beaver attained official status as an emblem of Canada when an "act to provide for the recognition of the beaver (castor canadensis) as a symbol of the sovereignty of Canada" received royal assent on March 24, 1975.

Today, thanks to conservation and silk hats, the beaver — the largest rodent in Canada — is alive and well all over the country.

Tartans

Maple Leaf
Approved for use in the Canadian Armed Forces on March 11, 1970.

Royal Canadian Air Force
Approved by the Court of Lord Lyon, King of Arms of Scotland, August 15, 1942.

CANADA

GOD SAVE THE QUEEN

God save our gracious Queen!
Long live our noble Queen!
God save the Queen!
Send her victorious,
Happy and glorious,
Long to reign over us,
God save the Queen!

DIEU PROTÈGE LA REINE

Dieu protège la Reine
De sa main souveraine!
Vive la Reine!
Qu'un règne glorieux,
Long et victorieux
Rende son peuple heureux.
Vive la Reine!

Royal Union Flag
(or Union Jack)

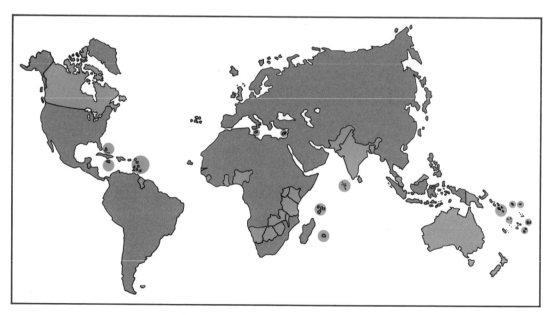

The Commonwealth

"God Save the Queen"

The anthem originated as a patriotic song in London, England, in 1745. Neither the author nor the composer is known. As the Royal Anthem of Canada, it is performed officially in Canada in the presence of members of the Royal Family, as part of the Salute accorded to the Governor General and Lieutenant Governors, and on other occasions.

Royal Union Flag

(or Union Jack)

Taking its present form from the Royal Flag of 1606, the original Union Flag first came into use in Canada with the British settlement in Nova Scotia after 1621. Following the *Act of Union* between Great Britain and Ireland in 1801, the Union Flag was proclaimed in its present form. In 1869, the Union Flag was incorporated into an official flag for the Lieutenant Governors of the provinces of Ontario, Quebec, Nova Scotia and New Brunswick.

The Union Flag was the affirmed national symbol from 1904 and was the flag under which Canadian troops fought during the First World War. On December 18, 1964, Parliament approved the continued use of the Union Flag as a symbol of Canada's membership in the Commonwealth of Nations and of her allegiance to The Crown.

Today, the Union Flag is to be flown along with the National Flag at federal buildings, airports and military bases on special occasions, such as The Queen's birthday, the anniversary of *The Statute of Westminster* (December 11), Commonwealth Day (second Monday in March) and during Royal Visits.

The Union Jack is prominent in the armorial bearings of the province of British Columbia and in the flags of the provinces of British Columbia, Ontario and Manitoba.

The Commonwealth

Fifty independent countries are members of the Commonwealth. This loose, voluntary association of Britain and most of her former colonies comprises a quarter of the world's nations — over one billion people.

Countries belong to the Commonwealth because they value it as an association. It spans all continents and forms a bridge between races and religions and between rich and poor. It enables people to discuss their common problems frankly and to work together in finding solutions.

With Confederation in 1867, Canada became the first federation in the British Empire. Its size, economic strength and seniority enabled it to become a leader in the widening of colonial autonomy and the transformation of the Empire into a Commonwealth of equal nations.

In a process of organic historic growth, the Commonwealth of today has succeeded the British Commonwealth (a title discarded in 1951), which in turn grew out of the old British Empire. The emergence of today's Commonwealth of equal partners, devoted to co-operation in the interests of freedom and development, began with the independence of the dominions of Canada, Australia, New Zealand and South Africa. Legal expression was given in *The Statute of Westminster* (1931).

The Commonwealth of today bears little resemblance to the Empire from which it grew. It began to take its modern form with the granting of independence to India in 1947. Two years later, India became a republic and the Commonwealth adapted itself to accept countries that owed no allegiance to the British Crown. All Commonwealth countries regard Queen Elizabeth II as a symbol of the association and as such the Head of the Commonwealth.

The Commonwealth has grown as former colonies in Asia, Africa, the Caribbean, the Mediterranean, and the Pacific were granted their independence and chose to remain members of the association. With a multiracial composition, the Commonwealth has become more representative of the world community and has increased in influence.

All members are equal within the association. Each is free to follow its own policies, but all subscribe to a set of common ideals agreed to by Commonwealth prime ministers and presidents in 1971. By adopting the Declaration of Commonwealth Principles, Commonwealth nations express their commitment to international peace and order, equal rights for all citizens, the liberty of the individual, opposing colonial domination and racial oppression, and a resolve to achieve a fairer global society.

In the last three decades, the Commonwealth has been active in hastening decolonization and promoting social and economic development. It has launched many programs of co-operation and works with other nations and groups in seeking to correct the imbalances between rich and poor countries.

Official Colours

History records that at the time of the first crusade, Bohémond I, a Norman lord, had red crosses cut from his cloak, which he distributed to 10,000 crusaders. The crusaders wore the crosses on their clothes as a distinguishing mark, since they had no uniform to indicate their identity.

In succeeding crusades, each nation was designated by a cross of a different colour. For a long time, France used a red cross on its banners, while England carried a white cross. In the course of history, red and white alternated as the national colours of France and England.

White and red were officially designated as the colours for Canada in the proclamation of the Royal Arms of Canada by King George V in 1921.

CANADA

HISTORICAL FLAGS

St. George's Cross

Fleur-de-lis

Royal Union Flag

(1606-1800)

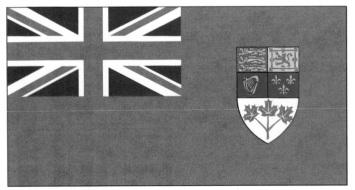

Canadian Red Ensign

St. George's Cross

This English flag of the 15th century was likely the first flag to fly over what is now Canada. The St. George's Cross was carried by John Cabot, a Venetian sailing under English colours, when he reached the east coast of Canada in 1497. The St. George's Cross is prominent in many provincial and territorial armorial bearings.

Fleur-de-lis

The fleur-de-lis was a symbol of French sovereignty in Canada from 1534, when Jacques Cartier landed and claimed the New World for France, until the *Treaty of Paris* in 1763, when Canada was ceded to the United Kingdom. Although a number of French military flags were used in Canada during this period, including the white flag of la marine royale after 1674, the fleur-de-lis held a position of some prominence. It reappeared as a symbol of French heritage in the arms granted to Quebec by Queen Victoria in 1868. In 1948, the Quebec government adopted the fleurdelisé as its provincial flag. It also appears in the armorial bearings of Canada and New Brunswick.

Royal Union Flag
(1606-1800)

Following the *Treaty of Paris* in 1763, the official British flag was the two-crossed jack or the Royal Union Flag. First proclaimed as a royal flag in 1606 after James VI of Scotland became James I of England, it combined England's flag of a red St. George's Cross on a white background with Scotland's flag, a white St. Andrew's Cross on a dark blue background. After the legislative union of England and Scotland in 1708, the Union Flag was adopted as the Royal Flag for the United Kingdom.

In the years between the *Treaty of Paris* and the American revolution, the Royal Union Flag was used at all British establishments on the North American continent from Newfoundland to the Gulf of Mexico. Following the revolution, those colonists who remained loyal to the crown and fought under this flag settled in many parts of what are now Ontario, New Brunswick and Nova Scotia. This flag is often referred to as the flag of Canada's United Empire Loyalists.

Following the *Act of Union* between Great Britain and Ireland in 1801, the diagonal Cross of St. Patrick, red on white, was incorporated and gave the Royal Union Flag its present-day configuration.

Canadian Red Ensign

The Red Ensign was created in 1707 as the flag of the British merchant marine. From approximately 1870 to 1904, it was used on land and sea as Canada's flag, with the quartered arms of Ontario, Quebec, Nova Scotia and New Brunswick in the fly. Although its use on land had never been authorized except by public sanction, in 1892 the British Admiralty approved the use of the Red Ensign for Canadian use at sea. This gave rise to the name 'the Canadian Red Ensign'.

As new provinces entered Confederation, or when they received some mark of identification, sometimes from their seal, the device was incorporated into the shield of the flag. By the turn of the century, the shield comprised the arms of the seven provinces then in Confederation. In 1924, this unofficial version of the Canadian Red Ensign was changed when, through an Order in Council, the Canadian government authorized the placing of the arms, granted in 1921 by King George V, in the fly of the flag. At this time, it was approved for use on Canadian government buildings abroad. A similar order in 1945 authorized its use on federal buildings within Canada until a new national flag was adopted.

The Canadian Red Ensign was replaced by the red and white maple leaf flag on February 15, 1965.

CANADA

HISTORICAL BOUNDARIES

1867

1870 to 1873

1874 to 1882

1884 to 1905

1912

1920 to 1949

Origin of the Name

The name Quebec comes from the Algonquin word for ''narrow passage'' or ''strait'' and was first used in reference to the narrowing of the St. Lawrence River near Quebec City. Quebec has had many names throughout its history: Canada, New France, Lower Canada and Canada East.

History

The original settlers were Indian tribes, mostly of the Algonquian and Iroquoian linguistic groups. They greatly influenced the early history of Quebec. Among the Algonquian tribes were the Naskapi-Montagnais and the Algonquin. The Iroquoian included the Seneca, Oneida, Onondaga, Cayuga and the Mohawk. Northern Quebec was, and largely is, inhabited by Inuit.

Quebec was one of the first areas in Canada to be explored and settled by Europeans. Jacques Cartier landed in the Gaspé in 1534, and claimed the land in the name of King François I of France.

After the *Treaty of Paris* in 1763, New France was ceded to the British, along with all the French colonies in Canada (except the islands of St. Pierre and Miquelon). An area including the former French colony and parts of present-day Ontario was renamed the Province of Quebec by the British.

In 1791, the province was divided into Upper and Lower Canada to accommodate the sudden influx of Loyalists from the American colonies to the western half of the province (present-day Ontario). After rebellions in both provinces in 1837, the two were reunited by the *Act of Union, 1840* and became the British Province of Canada.

However, the union was not successful. Canada East and Canada West, as they came to be known, retained their separate identities. Yet they knew that some kind of alliance was the best way of achieving greater independence from both Britain and the United States. When the province entered into the confederation agreement with Nova Scotia and New Brunswick in 1867, Canada East became the new Province of Quebec, and Canada West became the Province of Ontario.

The area of Quebec was increased first in 1898 and then in 1912, when its boundaries were redefined to include the District of Ungava, formerly part of the Northwest Territories. A boundary dispute between Canada and Newfoundland over the exact border between Labrador and Quebec was decided by the British Privy Council in 1927.

Quebec is the largest province in Canada. It is three times the size of France and seven times larger than Great Britain.

Date of Entry into Confederation

Quebec was among the first four provinces to form the Dominion of Canada at Confederation on July 1, 1867.

Armorial Bearing

Adopted:
Granted by Queen Victoria, May 26, 1868, and revised by Order of the Lieutenant Governor in Council, December 9, 1939.

Description:
The shield features three gold fleurs-de-lis on a blue field, a reminder of Royal France which once ruled Quebec. The original coat of arms, granted shortly after Confederation, had two blue fleurs-de-lis on a gold background. A sprig of three green maple leaves, thought to be representative of the most characteristic product of Quebec, is displayed in the lower portion. The gold lion in the centre third represents the British Crown that granted the shield.

Motto

JE ME SOUVIENS (*I remember*)

Flag

Adopted:
By Order of the Lieutenant Governor in Council on January 21, 1948; assented to by an Act of the Legislature on March 9, 1950.

Description:
Quebec's flag is generally known as the ''fleurdelisé'' flag. The white cross on a blue field recalls an ancient French military banner, and the four fleurs-de-lis are symbolic of France.

Proportion:
Three by length and two by width

Floral Emblem

Adopted:
March 13, 1963

Description:
The white garden lily, or madonna lily, of Quebec is the only official provincial/territorial flower that does not grow naturally in Canada. It was chosen as Quebec's emblem because of its resemblance to the fleur-de-lis, symbolic of France, the province's founding nation. The madonna lily is native to southeastern Europe and Asia Minor but can be cultivated in most parts of Eastern Canada and British Columbia. It is one of the most fragrant and beautiful members of the lily family.

Other Provincial Symbols

Tree: American Elm

Mineral: Asbestos

Bird: Snowy Owl

NOVA SCOTIA

Flag

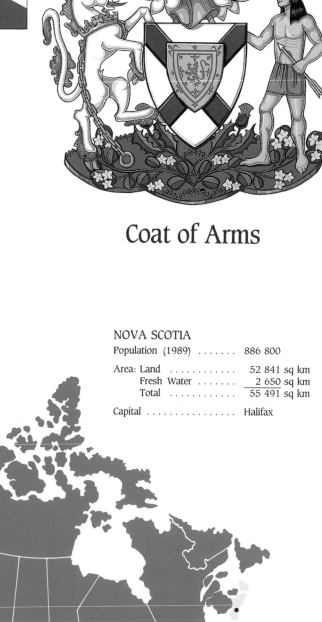

Coat of Arms

Floral Emblem
Mayflower

NOVA SCOTIA

Population (1989) 886 800

Area: Land . . . . 52 841 sq km
     Fresh Water . . . . 2 650 sq km
     Total . . . . 55 491 sq km

Capital . . . . Halifax

Origin of the Name

Nova Scotia was named by Sir William Alexander who, in 1621, received a grant to all the land between New England and Newfoundland from King James VI of Scotland (King James I of England). The official charter was in Latin and the name, ''New Scotland,'' retained its Latin form — *Nova Scotia*.

History

The Micmac Indians of the Algonquian linguistic group inhabited Nova Scotia long before the first explorers arrived from Europe. The Micmac were among the first natives to see Europeans. The Micmac allied themselves with the French throughout the early periods in Canadian history, helping them adjust to the land and fight against the British.

All of Nova Scotia, as well as parts of Quebec, New Brunswick and Maine, was originally known as Acadia and mainly settled by the French. Pierre de Monts established the first successful agricultural settlement in Canada, at Port-Royal (now Annapolis Royal) in 1605. For the next century, the British and the French feuded over the area. Control passed back and forth until 1713, when all of Acadia, except Cape Breton Island (then Îsle Royale), was ceded to the British under the *Treaty of Utrecht*.

Conflict between Britain and France continued. The Acadians tried to convince both sides of their neutrality but by 1755, just before the outbreak of the Seven Years War, the British decided the Acadians posed too great a security threat. They expelled all Acadians who would not swear allegiance to the British Crown. Many returned to France, some settled in New France and many others moved to the United States. Some who sided with the British chose to remain and they retained their land.

After the Seven Years War, the colony of Nova Scotia included Prince Edward Island, Cape Breton Island and the area now known as New Brunswick. In 1784, after a great influx of loyalist refugees from the United States, Nova Scotia was partitioned to create the colonies of New Brunswick and Cape Breton Island. However, Cape Breton again became part of Nova Scotia in 1820. Prince Edward Island had separated from Nova Scotia in 1769.

Although Nova Scotia was an original member of Confederation, there was a strong movement within the province to repeal the union. On July 1, 1867, some shops in Nova Scotia were hung with black crepe in mourning. For several years after, many Nova Scotians flew the flag at half mast on July 1.

Date of Entry into Confederation

Nova Scotia was among the first four provinces to form the Dominion of Canada at Confederation on July 1, 1867.

Armorial Bearings

Adopted:
A coat of arms was first granted in 1625. It was reinstated by royal warrant of King George V on January 19, 1929 to supersede the second coat of arms granted in May 1868.

Description:
The shield features the Scottish Cross of St. Andrew. To differentiate between the mother country and New Scotland, however, the colours of the cross are reversed: blue on white. At the centre is the inescutcheon of the Royal Arms of Scotland, containing a royal lion within a double red border on a field of yellow or gold.

In the crest are two hands, one armed and the other bare, supporting a laurel and a thistle. One interpretation of this has the armed hand and the thistle representing the vow of the King of the Scots to protect his subjects, and the bare hand and the laurel sprig representing the conquest of the difficulties to be met in Nova Scotia. The laurel sprig is a symbol of peace, triumph and conquest.

The crowned unicorn is one of the supporters of the shield, and is part of the royal armorial bearings of Scotland. The other supporter is an aboriginal, representing the native Indian population. Unlike the aboriginals that support the Newfoundland shield, this is a 17th century European representation.

A royal helmet — one that faces forward — rests on the shield. A feature of the Nova Scotia arms, unique among the provincial and territorial armorial bearings, is that the motto is placed above the arms, a common practice in Scotland.

Nova Scotia was the only province to have had a coat of arms annulled. When Nova Scotia joined Confederation, it was awarded a new coat of arms, just as were the other new provinces. Unlike the others, however, Nova Scotia had already been granted one. After the First World War, there was a movement to restore the old arms. This change received royal approval in 1929.

Motto

MUNIT HAEC ET ALTERA VINCIT (*One defends and the other conquers*)

Flag

Adopted:
The flag was first authorized by the Charter of New Scotland granted to Sir William Alexander by King James VI of Scotland (James I of England) in 1621. Nova Scotia was the first British colony to have its own flag by royal charter.

Description:
The flag consists of the shield extended in a rectangular shape.

Proportion:
Four by length and three by width

Floral Emblem

Adopted: April 1901

Description:
The mayflower, also known as trailing arbutus, blooms in the forest glades of early spring, often amid the last remaining snows of winter. The pink flowers are delicately scented and grow on stems from 15 to 30 cm long. It derives its name from the Pilgrims who saw it as the first flower of spring and named it after the ship that brought them to Plymouth Rock.

Other Provincial Symbols

Tartan: The Nova Scotia Tartan (the first provincial-territorial tartan in Canada; registered with the Court of the Lord Lyon, King of Arms of Scotland, 1956).
Tree: Red Spruce
Gemstone: Agate
Mineral: Stilbite

NEW BRUNSWICK

Flag

Coat of Arms

Floral Emblem
Purple Violet

NEW BRUNSWICK

Population (1989)	718 500
Area: Land	72 092 sq km
Fresh Water	1 344 sq km
Total	73 436 sq km
Capital	Fredericton

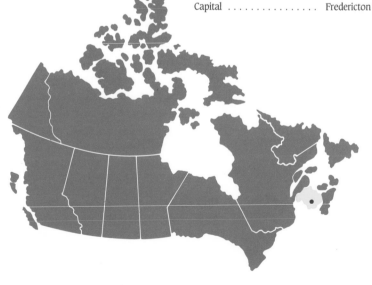

Origin of the Name

New Brunswick was named in 1784 to honour the reigning British monarch, King George III, who was also Duke of Brunswick and a member of the House of Hanover.

History

The area now known as New Brunswick was originally inhabited by tribes of the Algonquian linguistic group. The Micmacs welcomed the French under DeMonts and Samuel de Champlain when they first landed in New Brunswick in 1604. The relationship between the Indians and the French was good from the start. They helped the French settlers, who became known as Acadians, adapt to the land and helped the French launch raids on New England.

The Acadians, mainly settlers from France, were the first Europeans to settle in present-day New Brunswick. Until the *Treaty of Utrecht* in 1713, when France ceded the area to Great Britain, both Nova Scotia and New Brunswick were part of Acadia. However, over the years, France had all but ignored the Acadians, being much more concerned with New France and the increasing value of the fur trade there.

The *Treaty of Utrecht* created the British colony of Nova Scotia, which at that time included New Brunswick and Prince Edward Island. Nevertheless, Acadia continued for many years to be an area of conflict between the old world powers, falling eventually to Britain. As a consequence of the conflict, many Acadians fled while others were expelled by the Nova Scotian authorities in 1755. Before the peace of 1763, permanent British settlements, in what is now New Brunswick, were started by New Englanders at Chignecto and in the St. John River Valley. A trading community was established at the river's mouth by Massachusetts merchants in 1762 and settlers from Yorkshire, who came to Chignecto in the early 1770s, helped defeat an attempt from the rebellious colonies in 1776 to take Chignecto, and its strategic Fort Cumberland/Beauséjour.

In 1783, the western part of Nova Scotia received thousands of Loyalist refugees displaced by the American revolution. Their new lands were isolated from Halifax and, in 1784, the British government established the colony of New Brunswick in response to the Loyalists' demands.

In 1864, New Brunswick was involved in discussions with the colonies of Nova Scotia, Prince Edward Island and Newfoundland to consider a Maritime union when the Province of Canada issued an invitation to attend the conference in Charlottetown. The result, three years later, was the creation of the Dominion of Canada.

Date of Entry into Confederation

New Brunswick was among the first four provinces to form the Dominion of Canada at Confederation on July 1, 1867. Promises of increased prosperity, a railway linking New Brunswick to central Canada and a desire to unite with other British colonies to form a strong country against the influence of the United States, all encouraged New Brunswick to join.

Armorial Bearings

Adopted:
Shield of arms granted by royal warrant of Queen Victoria on May 26, 1868. Crest and supporters granted and motto confirmed by royal warrant of Queen Elizabeth II in 1984 to honour the 200th anniversary of the creation of New Brunswick.

Description:
The upper third of the shield is red and features a gold lion, symbolizing New Brunswick's ties to Britain. The lion is also found in the arms of the Duchy of Brunswick in Germany, the ancestral home of King George III. The lower part of the shield displays an ancient galley with oars in action. It could be interpreted as a reference to the importance of both shipbuilding and seafaring to New Brunswick in those days. It is also based on the design of the province's original great seal which featured a sailing ship on water.

The shield is supported by two white-tailed deer wearing collars of Indian wampum. From one is suspended the

Royal Union Flag (the Union Jack), from the other the fleur-de-lis to indicate the province's British and French background. The crest consists of an Atlantic salmon leaping from a coronet of gold maple leaves and bearing St. Edward's Crown on its back. The base, or compartment, is a grassy mound with fiddleheads as well as purple violets, the provincial floral emblem.

Motto

SPEM REDUXIT *(Hope restored)*. This is taken from the first great seal of the province.

Flag

Adopted:
The shield of arms assigned by Queen Victoria in 1868 was also authorized for use on flags and banners. The flag design was proclaimed by the Lieutenant Governor on February 24, 1965.

Description:
The flag is the province's shield of arms displayed throughout on a banner of rectangular form.

Proportion:
Four by length and two and one-half by width. The red portion with the lion occupies one-third the surface.

Floral Emblem

Adopted:
December 1, 1936

Description:
The purple violet, a relative of the pansy, can be purple or dark blue and is also known as the marsh blue violet. Its stems are from 8 to 15 cm long. The purple violet is found throughout Eastern Canada, particularly in wet meadows and woodlands. It grows especially well in New Brunswick and is seen in fields, lawns, and gardens in the early summer.

Other Provincial Symbols

Tartan: The New Brunswick Tartan

Tree: Balsam Fir

Bird: The Black-capped Chickadee

MANITOBA

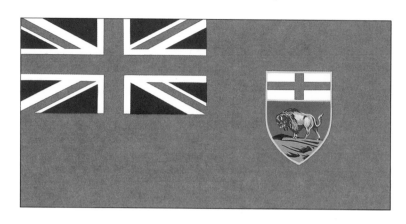

Flag

Coat of Arms

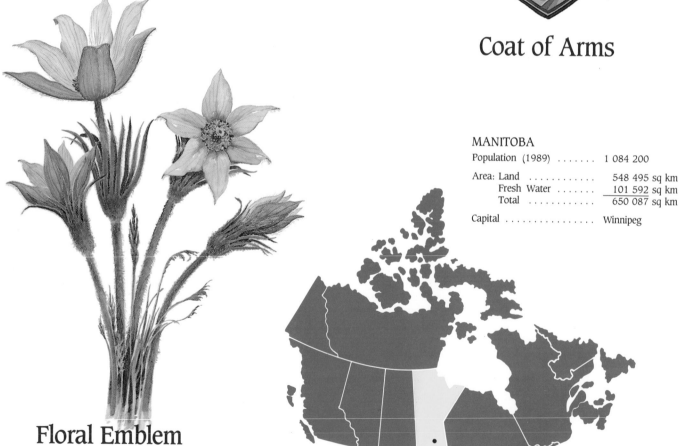

Floral Emblem
Prairie Crocus

MANITOBA

Population (1989) 1 084 200

Area: Land . . . . 548 495 sq km
      Fresh Water . . . . 101 592 sq km
      Total . . . . 650 087 sq km

Capital . . . . Winnipeg

THE TARTANS OF CANADA

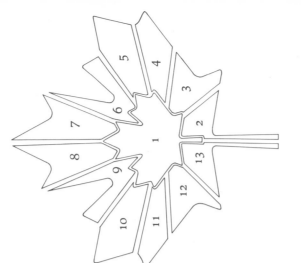

1 CANADA
2 NEWFOUNDLAND
3 PRINCE EDWARD ISLAND
4 NOVA SCOTIA
5 NEW BRUNSWICK
6 QUEBEC
7 ONTARIO
8 MANITOBA
9 SASKATCHEWAN
10 ALBERTA
11 BRITISH COLUMBIA
12 NORTHWEST TERRITORIES
13 YUKON

Canada

The Floral Emblems of Canada

1 ONTARIO – *White Trillium*
2 QUEBEC – *White Garden Lily*
3 NOVA SCOTIA – *Mayflower*
4 NEW BRUNSWICK – *Purple Violet*
5 MANITOBA – *Prairie Crocus*
6 BRITISH COLUMBIA – *Pacific Dogwood*
7 PRINCE EDWARD ISLAND – *Lady's-Slipper*
8 SASKATCHEWAN – *Red Lily*
9 ALBERTA – *Wild Rose*
10 NEWFOUNDLAND – *Pitcher Plant*
11 NORTHWEST TERRITORIES – *Mountain Avens*
12 YUKON – *Fireweed*

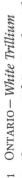

**Department of the Secretary   Secrétariat d'État
of State of Canada   du Canada**

Origin of the Name

The name Manitoba likely comes from the Cree words "Manitou bou", which means "the narrows of the Great Spirit." It applied to Lake Manitoba that narrows to half a mile at the centre. The waves on the loose surface rocks of its north shore produce curious bell-like and wailing sounds, which the first Indian visitors believed came from a huge drum beaten by the spirit Manitou. The name was given to the province on its creation in 1870 at the suggestion of Louis Riel.

History

The Assiniboine Indians were the first inhabitants of Manitoba. Other tribes included the nomadic Cree, who followed the herds of buffalo and caribou on their seasonal migrations.

In their search for the spice-rich Orient through the Northwest Passage, Europeans reached Manitoba through Hudson Bay. Unlike most of the rest of Canada, the northern parts of the province were settled before the south. In 1612, Captain Thomas Button wintered two ships at Port Nelson on Hudson Bay, near the mouths of the Nelson and Hayes Rivers. In 1690 and 1691, Henry Kelsey explored northern Manitoba from Hudson Bay as far as the Saskatchewan River, near The Pas. A party led by La Verendrye explored the Red and Winnipeg Rivers in the years 1733-38 and built several outposts.

In 1670, King Charles II of England granted the Hudson's Bay Company a large tract of land named Rupert's Land. The company set up fur-trading posts to exploit the country's wealth. Among their major posts were York Factory at the mouths of the Nelson and Hayes Rivers, and Fort Prince of Wales at the mouth of the Churchill River. The latter was a large stone fort, built between the years 1731-71, captured and badly damaged by the French in 1782. The Hudson's Bay Company then built Fort Churchill in 1783 and continued to use that site until 1933.

After 1740, in the wake of La Verendrye, traders from New France pushed across the southern part of Manitoba. They were later replaced by teams of English-speaking "pedlars" and French-Canadian voyageurs who drove swift canoes from Montreal to the West and back, seeking furs.

Intense rivalry for furs developed between the Montreal-based North West Company and the Hudson's Bay Company. Their battle for the fur trade resulted in both companies building forts throughout the plains. Alexander Mackenzie, an employee of the North West Company, pushed the chain of forts into the Rocky Mountains and the Arctic. The rivalry came to its height in the Red River and Assiniboine River Valleys in Manitoba, where open warfare broke out.

During the same period, the first European agricultural settlement was established by Lord Selkirk, a Scottish nobleman, who sent a number of dispossessed Scottish Highlanders to settle land he had secured from the Hudson's Bay Company in 1811. He called the area Assiniboia.

The Selkirk colony was also caught in the fur-trade war and, in 1816, Governor Robert Semple and 19 colonists were killed at Seven Oaks in a battle with the Metis, who had been urged on by the North West Company. However, the settlement survived and its permanent way of life materially affected the semi-nomadic way of life of the Red River Valley. The violence and lengthy legal battles brought about the bankruptcy of the company and the impoverishment of Selkirk.

In the 1860s, the Province of Canada, anxious to expand into the great northwest, asked Britain to buy out the Hudson's Bay Company as it had the East India Company. Although willing to request the surrender of the land from the Hudson's Bay Company, Britain insisted that the money come from Canada. Canada offered the company 300,000 pounds sterling. The company settled for the money, plus one-twentieth of all the fertile land in the west and the land that surrounded their trading posts.

The inhabitants of the area were not consulted on this transaction. This lack of consultation, plus the constant threat from the south of an American invasion, made them nervous. No clear terms were spelled out for the people of the Red River area and, during negotiations on their status, resistance developed in the colony. The Metis, a mostly French-speaking people of white and Indian blood, under the leadership of Louis Riel opposed the Canadian proposals. Riel succeeded in uniting both the French and English-speaking groups and established a locally-elected, provisional government in December 1869.

Delegates of this provisional government negotiated terms with the federal government that led to Parliament passing the *Manitoba Act*, May 12, 1870, under which Manitoba joined the other provinces in Confederation. The Act was proclaimed, making Manitoba a province of the Dominion of Canada, on July 15, 1870.

The new "postage stamp" province consisted of 36,000 km^2 surrounding the Red River Valley. It was called the postage stamp province because of its square shape and small size.

However, the province did not remain that small. Its boundaries were stretched in 1881 and again in 1912. It is now 650,000 km^2 and could have been larger had it not been for an 1884 decision in favour of Ontario, which established the boundary between the two provinces.

Agricultural settlement helped the province prosper in its infancy. With the help of the railway and certain Acts of Parliament in the late 1800s, the province was soon filled with settlers from Eastern Canada and Europe.

Date of Entry into Confederation

The Province of Manitoba was created and joined the Dominion of Canada on July 15, 1870 by the *Manitoba Act*.

Armorial Bearings

Adopted:
Received approval from the federal government in 1870, soon after joining Confederation. Granted by royal warrant of King Edward VII on May 10, 1905.

Description:
The top part of the shield features the Cross of St. George, taken from the arms of the Hudson's Bay Company. The lower part shows a buffalo standing on a rock. The buffalo once roamed in this area by the thousands and played a prominent role in the province's early history. The use of an entire buffalo in the shield is unique in heraldry. Although the buffalo is a common symbol, especially in central Europe, usually only the head is used.

Flag

Adopted:
May 12, 1966, by warrant of Queen Elizabeth II

Description:
The flag closely resembles the Canadian Red Ensign. The Union Jack occupies the upper quarter on the staff side, while the provincial shield is centred on the fly half of the flag.

Proportion:
Two by length and one by width

Floral Emblem

Adopted:
March 16, 1906

Description:
The prairie crocus is an early spring flower often seen pushing through the last prairie snow. The flowers range from light lavender to bluish purple and wear an outer coating of hair to protect them from sudden changes in temperature. Manitoba was the first prairie province to adopt a floral emblem, and the prairie crocus was chosen in an informal vote in the province's schools.

Other Provincial Symbols

Tartan: The Manitoba Tartan

Tree: White Spruce

Bird: Great Gray Owl

BRITISH COLUMBIA

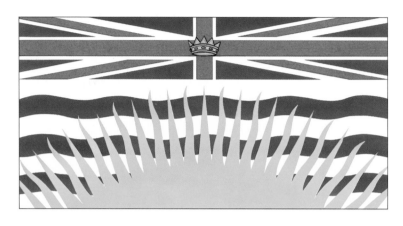

Flag

Coat of Arms

BRITISH COLUMBIA

Population (1989)		3 055 600
Area: Land		930 528 sq km
Fresh Water		18 068 sq km
Total		948 596 sq km
Capital		Victoria

Floral Emblem
Pacific Dogwood

Origin of the Name

The southern region of the area now known as British Columbia was called Columbia, after the Columbia River, and the central region was given the name of New Caledonia by Simon Fraser as he explored the area. To avoid confusion with Colombia in South America and the island of New Caledonia in the Pacific, Queen Victoria named the area British Columbia when it became a colony in 1858.

History

British Columbia was inhabited by the greatest number of distinct Indian tribes of any province or territory in Canada. Because of the diversity of the Pacific coast — mild to cold climates, seashore to mountain tops — the tribes that settled in this area developed completely different cultures and languages. Experts have found very few similarities among their languages. They were not only different from each other, but also from the rest of the Indian tribes in Canada. Among the tribes along the coastline were the Nootka, Bella Coola, Tlinkit, Haida, Tsimshian, Kwakiutl and Salish. The tribes found on the plateaus of the Rocky Mountains included the Tagish, Tahltan, Tsetsaut, Carrier, Chilcotin, Interior Salish, Nicola and Kootenay.

Unlike Eastern Canada, where the French and English disputed control of the land, the first two countries to contest areas of British Columbia were Spain and Russia. In the 1700s, the Spanish claimed ownership of the west coast from Mexico to Vancouver Island. At the same time, the Russians were making an overlapping claim: control of the Pacific coast from Alaska to San Francisco.

In 1778, Captain James Cook of Great Britain became the first person to actually chart the land. George Vancouver, a 20-year-old midshipman on Cook's voyage, later led three expeditions of his own and charted more than 16,000 km of the coastline. Having firmly established her right to the area, Britain proceeded to settle disputes with both Spain and Russia.

The 1846 *Oregon Treaty* with the United States gave Britain sole ownership of Vancouver Island and the area north of the 49th parallel. In 1849, Vancouver Island was granted to the Hudson's Bay Company in the hope that it might be settled. Until that time, the only European settlements in that part of the country were fur-trading posts.

When gold was discovered in the lower Fraser Valley in 1857, thousands of people came in search of instant wealth. To help maintain law and order, the next year the British government established the separate colony of British Columbia. In 1866, when the frenzy of the gold rush was over, the colony of Vancouver Island joined the colony of British Columbia.

The colony was cut off from the rest of British North America by thousands of kilometres, and a ridge of mountains. The promise of a rail link between the Pacific coast and the rest of Canada convinced British Columbia to join Confederation in 1871.

Date of Entry into Confederation

In 1871, British Columbia became the sixth province to join the Dominion of Canada.

Armorial Bearings

Adopted:
Shield granted by King Edward VII on March 31, 1906. Complete Coat of Arms granted in person by Her Majesty Queen Elizabeth II in a ceremony in the Vancouver Law Courts on October 15, 1987.

Description:
The Union Jack, with an antique golden crown in the centre, occupies the upper third of the shield, symbolizing the Province's origin as a British colony. The bottom of the shield features a golden half-sun, superimposed upon three wavy blue bars cast horizontally on white. The blue bars represent the Pacific Ocean and the sun signifies British Columbia's location as the most westerly province in Canada. The shield was designed by Victoria Clergyman Arthur Beanlands.

The shield is supported by a Wapiti Stag and a Bighorn Sheep Ram representing the Colonies of Vancouver Island and British Columbia.

The crest consists of a lion standing on a crown. The lion wears a garland of dogwoods around its neck, thus differentiating it from the Royal Crest. Between the crest and shield is placed the golden helmet of sovereignty, as a mark of British Columbia's co-sovereign status in Confederation. Above the helmet are the traditional heraldic elements of a wreath and mantling in red and white, the colours of Canada.

The provincial flower is featured a second time by entwining dogwoods around the motto scroll.

Motto

SPLENDOR SINE OCCASU (*Splendor without diminishment*)

Flag

Adopted:
King Edward VII assigned Arms and Banner on March 31, 1906. Flag adopted by Order of the Lieutenant Governor in Council on June 27, 1960.

Description:
The design of the flag duplicates the shield in the shape of a rectangle.

Proportion:
Five by length and three by width

Floral Emblem

Adopted:
1956

Description:
The Pacific dogwood is a tree that grows from 6 to 18 metres high and flowers profusely in April and May with white blossoms 10-13 cm across. The Pacific dogwood is also conspicuous in autumn with its clusters of bright red berries and brilliant foliage.

Other Provincial Symbols

Tartan: The British Columbia Tartan
Tree: Western Red Cedar
Gemstone: Jade
Bird: Steller's Jay

PRINCE EDWARD ISLAND

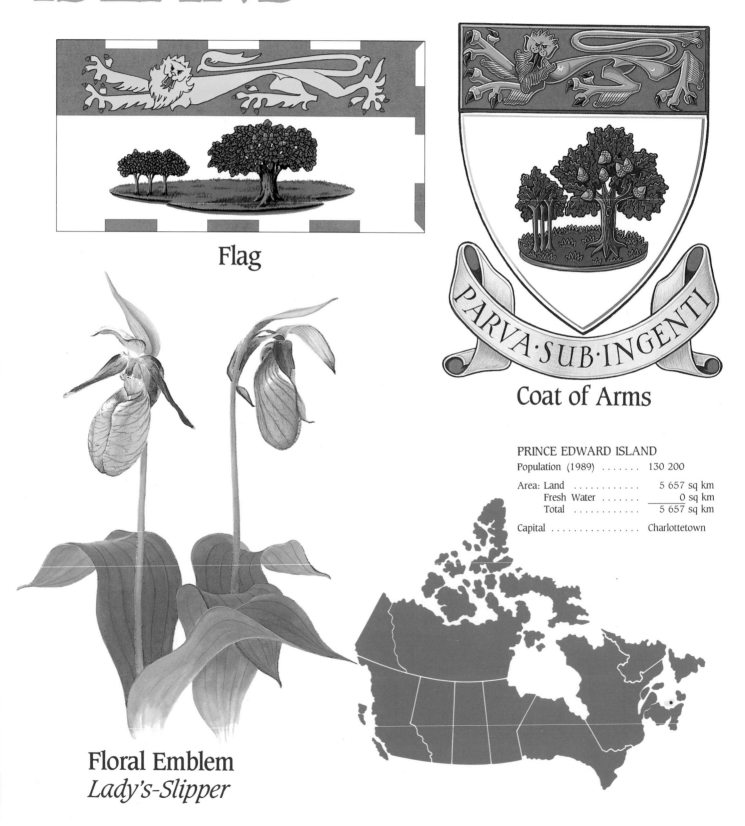

Flag

Coat of Arms

PARVA·SUB·INGENTI

Floral Emblem
Lady's-Slipper

PRINCE EDWARD ISLAND

Population (1989)		130 200
Area: Land		5 657 sq km
Fresh Water		0 sq km
Total		5 657 sq km
Capital		Charlottetown

Origin of the Name

The province's name was adopted in 1799 to honour a son of King George III: Prince Edward, Duke of Kent. The Prince, who was Queen Victoria's father, was commander-in-chief of British North America and was stationed in Halifax when the Island was named.

Previously, Prince Edward Island was called "Abegweit", derived from the Micmac "Abahquit" meaning "lying parallel with the land", often rendered loosely as "cradled in the waves". Early French settlers called it Isle Saint Jean and, when the *Treaty of Paris* in 1763 gave the Island to the British, the name was translated to St. John's Island.

The Island also has several nicknames, including the "Million-Acre Farm" and "The Garden of the Gulf."

History

Although the Micmac Indians have inhabited the Island for the last 2,000 years, there are indications that their ancestors lived there as long as 10,000 years ago. These native people are said to have reached the Island by crossing the low plain now covered by Northumberland Strait.

Europeans first discovered the Island when Jacques Cartier reached this "fairest land that may possibly be seen" in 1534. Despite such glowing reports, settlement of the Island was slow. Not until the early 1700s did the French establish a permanent colony and, by 1748, the population was still less than 700.

However, following the British expulsion of the Acadians from Nova Scotia in 1755, the population of the Island grew dramatically. When Louisbourg fell to the British in 1758, the population was more than 5,000. At that time, the British forced all but a few hundred of the Acadians to leave the island, even though France did not cede the Island until the *Treaty of Paris* in 1763.

In 1758, the Island became part of the British colony of Nova Scotia, which at that time also included the present-day province of New Brunswick. In 1769, it became a separate colony.

Prince Edward Island was plagued throughout most of the colonial period with problems of absentee landowners. Most of the people granted land by the British Crown never set foot on the Island. Some refused to sell land to the tenants; others charged outrageous prices to sell, or demanded high rents of those who wished to establish farms on the rich land.

The government of the Island attempted to impose a tax on land-owners to cover the cost of administration, but this tax was next to impossible to collect. In 1840, the colony was able to buy land from some of the landlords and make it available for purchase by tenants. Money for this purpose, however, was soon exhausted.

Prince Edward Island was host to the first of the confederation conferences in 1864. However, it dropped out of the discussions after the Quebec Conference in the fall of 1864 when it was felt that the Island's autonomy would be jeopardized by joining a large Canadian union.

That decision was overturned in 1873. The debt incurred in building a railway for the Island, pressure from the British government, and the attractive promises of the Canadian government pushed the Island into Confederation. The promises included an absorption of the debt, year-round communication with the mainland and funds to buy out the absentee landowners. Most islanders saw it as a marriage of necessity.

Date of Entry into Confederation

Prince Edward Island was not party to the 1867 agreement. The Charlotte-town Conference was originally planned as a forum to discuss a maritime union of Newfoundland, Nova Scotia, New Brunswick and Prince Edward Island. P.E.I. became a province of the Dominion of Canada in 1873.

Armorial Bearings

Adopted:
Granted officially by royal warrant of King Edward VII on May 30, 1905, though used on the provincial great seal since 1769.

Description:
The top segment of the shield features the English heraldic lion. The lion appears on the coat of arms of Prince Edward, after whom the Island was named, and on the royal coat of arms of King Edward VII, who assigned the provincial arms. The lower part of the shield shows a green island with a large oak tree on the right and three young oaks on the left. Symbolism: the mature tree is the Oak of England and the tree saplings represent the Province's three counties — King's, Queen's and Prince. The trees rise from a single base, both Britain and P.E.I. being islands.

Motto

PARVA SUB INGENTI *(the small under the protection of the great)*

Flag

Adopted:
March 24, 1964 by an Act of the Legislature

Description:
The design of the flag is modelled after the coat of arms in rectangular shape and is bordered on the three sides away from the mast by alternate bands of red and white.

Proportion:
Three in length and two in width. For a flag 183 cm (six feet) long, the alternating strips of the border are each 25.4 cm (10 inches) across.

Floral Emblem

Adopted:
April 25, 1947

Description:
The lady's-slipper (*Cypripedium acaule*) is a species of orchid. It gets its name from the shape of its petals which form a pouch somewhat like a slipper. Bees tumble into the pouch and, in their efforts to scramble out, brush against the male and female flower parts, thus pollinating the flowers. The lady's-slipper blooms in late May and June and grows in shady and moist woodlands.

Other Provincial Symbols

Tartan: The Prince Edward Island Tartan
Bird: Blue Jay

SASKATCHEWAN

Flag

Coat of Arms

Floral Emblem
Western Red Lily

SASKATCHEWAN

Population (1989) 1 007 000

Area: Land	. . . .	570 269 sq km
Fresh Water	. . . .	82 631 sq km
Total	. . . .	652 900 sq km

Capital . . . . Regina

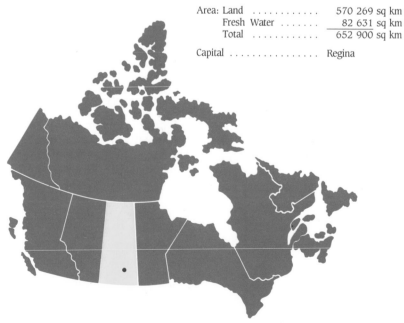

Origin of the Name

The Cree name for the Saskatchewan River was "Kisiskatchewanisipi," meaning "swift-flowing river." Through use, this eight-syllable name was shortened to Saskatchewan and, in 1882, it became the name of one of the districts of the Northwest Territories.

History

Saskatchewan was originally inhabited by Indian tribes of the Athabaskan, Algonquian and Siouan linguistic groups. Three Athabaskan tribes live in the north: the Chipewyan, the Beaver and the Slavey. Two Algonquian tribes — the Cree and the Blackfoot — occupied the central part of the province. The south was inhabited predominantly by the Siouan tribes — the Assiniboine and the Gros Ventres. The influence of native peoples in Saskatchewan is evident from the great variety of Indian place names.

Because the prairie, which makes up much of the province, was of little monetary interest to the early fur traders, southern Saskatchewan was relatively untouched by Europeans for many years. However, the northern wooded regions were dotted with furtrading posts early in Canadian history. The earliest explorer was Henry Kelsey, an employee of the Hudson's Bay Company, who in about 1690 followed the Saskatchewan River into the plains of Saskatchewan.

Both Britain and the Province of Canada sent out explorers in the mid-1800s to explore the area and assess its agricultural potential. After the *Dominion Lands Act* of 1872, which encouraged homesteaders, and an act to stimulate immigration, the new railway began bringing settlers who farmed this rich area.

In 1905, the Province of Saskatchewan was formed by joining the Districts of Saskatchewan and parts of the Districts of Athabaska and Assiniboia. It became the only province with artificial boundaries, not based on any particular geographical features. Alberta and Saskatchewan are the only Canadian provinces that are not bordered by salt water.

Saskatchewan grows two-thirds of Canada's wheat and is one of the world's greatest wheat producers. It has been nicknamed "Canada's breadbasket."

There are a number of colourful place names in Saskatchewan, among them Antler, Eyebrow, Moose Jaw, Drinkwater, Love, Conquest, Swift Current, Peebles, Squaw Rapids, Old Wives Lake and Grandmother's Bay. Other place names such as Fort Qu'appelle, Fond-du-lac, Bien Fait and Lac La Ronge, remind Canadians of the early French explorers who settled in the area long before the great wave of immigration from Eastern Europe in the late 1800s and early 1900s.

Date of Entry into Confederation

The area now known as Saskatchewan joined Confederation as a part of the Northwest Territories in 1870. It became a province of the Dominion of Canada on September 1, 1905.

Armorial Bearings

Adopted:
Shield of Arms granted by royal warrant of King Edward VII on August 25, 1906. Crest, supporters and motto granted by royal warrant of Queen Elizabeth II on September 16, 1986.

Description:
The shield of arms displays a red lion, a traditional royal symbol, on a horizontal gold band across the upper third; three gold wheat sheaves on a green background, symbolizing Saskatchewan's agriculture and resources, occupy the lower two-thirds.

The shield is supported by a royal lion and a white-tailed deer, an animal indigenous to Saskatchewan. Both supporters wear collars of Prairie Indian beadwork, from which are suspended badges in the form of the six-pointed star (stylized lily) of the Saskatchewan Award of Merit. The badge worn by the lion displays Canada's emblem, the maple leaf; that worn by the deer displays Saskatchewan's official flower, the western red lily.

Immediately above the shield is a helm (or helmet) facing left, representing the co-sovereign status of the province in Confederation. The helm is decorated with mantling. Above the helm is a wreath which supports a beaver — Canada's national animal — representing the North, the fur trade and the native people. The beaver holds a western red lily, the floral emblem of the province. The beaver is surmounted by the Crown, symbol of Saskatchewan's direct link with The Sovereign through the Lieutenant Governor.

Motto

MULTIS E GENTIBUS VIRES
(From Many Peoples Strength)

Flag

Adopted:
By Legislative Assembly on March 31, 1969. Proclaimed by the Lieutenant Governor on September 22, 1969.

Description:
The flag is divided horizontally into two equal parts, one green, the other gold. The green represents the northern forested areas of the province and the gold symbolizes the southern grain field areas. The shield of arms of Saskatchewan is in the upper quarter near the staff, and the provincial floral emblem, the western red lily, is positioned on the fly half of the flag. It is inspired by a design by Anthony Drake, which was chosen as a result of a provincial design competition.

Proportion:
Two by length and one by width

Floral Emblem

Adopted:
April 8, 1941

Description:
The western red lily grows in moist meadows and semi-wooded areas. It stands out brilliantly with its flaming red blossoms against a natural green background. The western red lily is now a protected species.

Other Provincial Symbols

Tartan: The Saskatchewan District Tartan (registered with the Court of the Lord Lyon, King of Arms of Scotland, 1961).

Tree: White Birch

Plant: Wheat (sheaf)

Bird: Sharp-tailed Grouse

ALBERTA

Flag

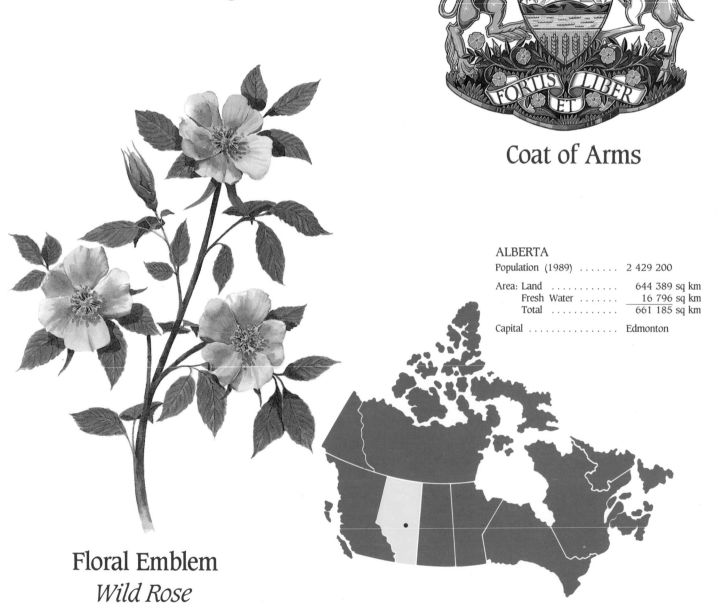

Coat of Arms

Floral Emblem
Wild Rose

ALBERTA

Population (1989) 2 429 200

Area: Land . . . . 644 389 sq km
      Fresh Water . . . . 16 796 sq km
      Total . . . . 661 185 sq km

Capital . . . . Edmonton

Origin of the Name

Alberta was named for Queen Victoria's fourth daughter, Princess Louise Caroline Alberta, the wife of the Marquis of Lorne. The Marquis was Governor General of Canada when the district was formed in 1882.

History

The Blackfoot, Blood, Peigan, Cree, Gros Ventre, Sarcee, Kootenay, Beaver and Slavey Indians were the first people to live in present-day Alberta. The first European explorer to reach what is now Alberta was Anthony Henday, in 1754. Peter Pond, of the North West Company, established the first fur-trading post in that area in 1778. From that time, the region was fought over by the Hudson's Bay Company and the North West Company, each of which built fur-trading posts. The fighting ended only in 1821, when the two companies merged.

Expeditions led by Henry Youle Hind and John Palliser found parts of the region to have exceptionally good farming land, especially the fertile belt north of the Palliser Triangle. As a result of these findings, the British decided not to renew the licence of the Hudson's Bay Company and, by 1870, the land of the northwest was acquired by the Dominion of Canada.

By 1881, however, there were barely more than 1,000 non-native people in the area that was to become the Province of Alberta. However, the population grew quickly, beginning with the arrival of the railway. In 1885, the CPR had reached Calgary and, by 1891, the Calgary & Edmonton Railway (now the CNR) was in Edmonton. Other factors that helped swell the population were the discovery of new strains of wheat particularly suited to the climate of the Canadian Prairies, the lack of new farmland in the United States, and the end of an economic depression throughout North America.

By 1891, 17,500 people were in the area and, by 1901, there were 73,022. By the end of the Canadian Government's immigration push in 1921, the population had reached 584,454. As a result, Alberta is made up of many peoples of different backgrounds, languages and cultures.

The present-day province was created in 1905 by joining the District of Alberta with parts of the Districts of Athabaska, Assiniboia and Saskatchewan.

Date of Entry into Confederation

The area now known as Alberta entered Confederation as part of the Northwest Territories in 1870. Both Alberta and its neighbour, Saskatchewan, became provinces of the Dominion of Canada in 1905. For the first time, Canadian provinces were joined from sea to sea.

Armorial Bearings

Adopted:
Granted by royal warrant of King Edward VII on May 30, 1907. Augmented with crest, supporters and motto on July 30, 1980, the 75th anniversary of the province's creation.

Description:
The upper portion of the shield displays the Cross of St. George, while a beaver is found in the crest. The lower part of the shield gives a picture of the nature of the land in the province — mountains, foothills, prairie and grain fields.

Growing at the base of the shield is the floral emblem of the province: the wild rose. The shield is supported by a lion and a pronghorned antelope.

Motto

FORTIS ET LIBER (*Strong and free*)

Flag

Adopted:
Although first used in 1967, it was proclaimed into force June 1, 1968, following an act of the Legislature.

Description:
The flag is based on Alberta's shield, and consists of the arms of the province on a royal ultramarine blue background.

Proportion:
Two by length and one by width, with the arms seven-elevenths the width of the flag and displayed in the centre.

Floral Emblem

Adopted: 1930

Description:
The wild rose, also known as the prickly rose, is the most widely distributed native rose in Canada, ranging from Quebec to British Columbia. Its colour and fragrance make it popular with people, and birds find its scarlet berries a valuable source of winter food. The wild rose was chosen as the provincial floral emblem by the school children of Alberta.

Other Provincial Symbols

Tartan: The Alberta Tartan

Tree: Lodgepole Pine

Stone: Petrified Wood

Bird: Great Horned Owl

Mammal: Rocky Mountain Big Horn Sheep

Colours: Blue and Gold

NEWFOUNDLAND

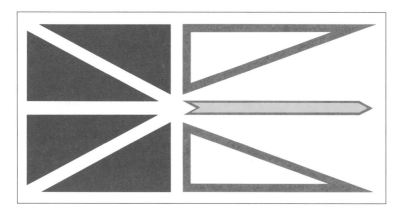

Flag

Coat of Arms

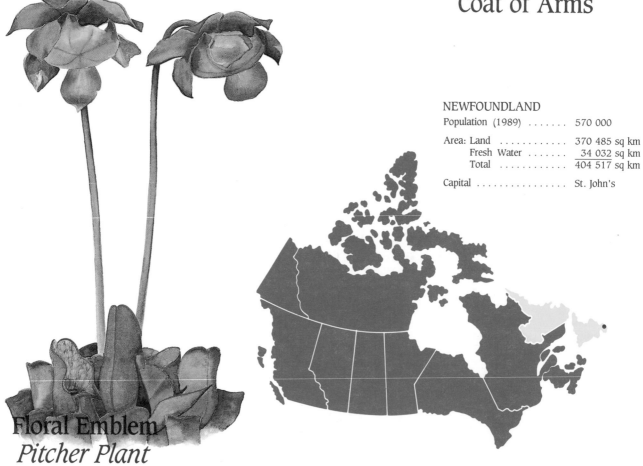

Floral Emblem
Pitcher Plant

NEWFOUNDLAND

Population (1989)	570 000
Area: Land	370 485 sq km
Fresh Water	34 032 sq km
Total	404 517 sq km
Capital	St. John's

Origin of the Name

King Henry VII of England referred to the land discovered by John Cabot in 1497 as the ''New Found Launde.'' Recently, some historians have proposed that the ''new isle'' Cabot discovered was Cape Breton Island, not Newfoundland.

History

The aboriginal inhabitants of Newfoundland were the Beothuk Indians. By the early 1800s, disease and conflicts with settlers and others frequenting the Island reduced the Beothuk to extinction.

There were, and still are, a relatively large number of Inuit concentrated in the coastal communities of Northern Labrador.

The first Europeans to visit Newfoundland were Norsemen who arrived around the 10th century. Other early visitors, the Basques, Portuguese, Spanish, British and French, staged fishing expeditions in the 16th century and probably earlier.

The Genoese navigator Giovanni Caboto, known to us as John Cabot, landed on the island on June 24, 1497, on the feast of St. John the Baptist. Cabot called the new land ''St. John's Isle'' in honour of the saint and claimed it for Henry VII of England, his patron and employer.

In 1583, Sir Humphrey Gilbert took formal possession of the Island of Newfoundland and the surrounding seas for Queen Elizabeth I.

In 1610, under a Royal Patent and grant of all of the Island of Newfoundland by King James I, a group of merchants tried to establish a permanent colony at what is now Cupids in Conception Bay. This has been considered the first recorded formal attempt to establish a permanent year-round settlement in Newfoundland.

Anglo-French colonial warfare shaped the history of Newfoundland during the 1600s and 1700s. France, already well-established on the mainland of Eastern Canada, began to make claims to parts of Newfoundland. In 1662, France established a fort and colony at Placentia, despite protests from British merchants and fishermen. The *Treaty of Utrecht* in 1713 ended a long period of raids and skirmishes by both nations, and reconfirmed British sovereignty over Newfoundland and the fishing banks.

The Seven Years War (1756-63) witnessed a repetition of the events from 1662 to 1713. In 1763, with the signing of the *Treaty of Paris*, British sovereignty was again recognized.

The people of Newfoundland were granted the right to vote for an elected assembly in 1832. Conflict between the assembly and the appointed council led to the collapse of the colonial government by 1841. In 1847, the British government decided to revert to a separate assembly and council, although the council was not made responsible to the assembly for its action. After much debate, Newfoundland was finally given responsible government in 1855.

Newfoundland sent observers to the confederation conference in Quebec City in 1864. In 1865, the colony postponed the decision on whether or not to join the union. Confederation became the major issue in the general election in Newfoundland in 1869, but the concept did not gain popular approval.

The Great Depression, combined with other factors, forced the government into bankruptcy by 1933. Newfoundland, a Dominion within the Commonwealth, asked the British government to suspend the legislature. Until 1949, a governor and a six-member Commission of Government ruled.

Following World War II, the question of Newfoundland's future status had become an issue once again. It was decided, through a convention, to hold a public referendum on the subject.

At first the convention decided on only two options: retention of the Commission of Government or a return to the 1934 status as a Dominion within the Commonwealth. However, a vigorous popular movement forced the British authorities to include a third option on the referendum in 1948: union with Canada. Following two referenda, Confederation with Canada won with 52 percent of the vote.

Date of Entry into Confederation

On March 31, 1949, Newfoundland, Britain's oldest colony, became the tenth province of the Dominion of Canada.

Armorial Bearings

Adopted:
Granted by King Charles I on January 1, 1638.

Description:
The shield is divided into four parts by a silver cross. This cross is reminiscent of the cross on the Arms of the Knights of St. John. John Cabot discovered the island on the feast of St. John in 1497. The first and fourth quarters show lions looking outward, and the second and third quarters display unicorns. These represent the supporters of the Royal Arms after the union of England and Scotland.

Two aboriginals in warlike clothing, representations of local natives, support the shield.

The elk in the crest was included as an example of the fauna of Newfoundland, but the elk has never been native to the province. It is possible that the animal was meant to be a caribou.

Motto

QUAERITE PRIME REGNUM DEI (*Seek ye first the Kingdom of God*)

Flag

Adopted:
Act of Legislature assented to May 28, 1980

Description:
The white symbolizes snow and ice; blue, the sea; red, human effort; and gold, confidence in the future. The two red triangles on the right stand for the mainland and island parts of the province, and the golden arrow represents hope for the future. The image of the trident on the flag emphasizes Newfoundland's continued dependence on fishing and the sea. When the flag is hung as a banner, the arrow assumes the aspect of a sword, a reminder of the sacrifices made in war.

Proportion:
Two by length and one by width

Floral Emblem

Adopted:
June 22, 1954

Description:
The insect-eating pitcher plant is the most unusual of Canada's official flowers. It was first chosen as a symbol of Newfoundland by Queen Victoria, to be engraved on the newly-minted, Newfoundland penny. It was used on the island's coinage until 1938. In 1954, the pitcher plant was declared the official emblem of the province.

Other Provincial Symbols

Gemstone: Labradorite

NORTHWEST TERRITORIES

Flag

Coat of Arms

Floral Emblem
Mountain Avens

NORTHWEST TERRITORIES

Population (1989)	53 400
Area: Land	3 246 390 sq km
Fresh Water	133 294 sq km
Total	3 379 684 sq km
Capital	Yellowknife

Origin of the Name

Most of today's Northwest Territories was known as the North-Western Territory until 1870. Then as now, the name is primarily descriptive of the location of the Territories.

History

The Northwest Territories were inhabited by Inuit and Indian tribes long before the Europeans started looking for the elusive Northwest Passage. Native Inuit included the MacKenzie, Copper, Caribou and Central tribes. There were also many Indian tribes when the Europeans first arrived, among them the Yellow-Knife, Chipewyan, Sekani, Beaver, Nahanni, Dogrib and Slavey. Some Indian tribes in the area spoke a form of the Athabaskan language, the only native language in North America to have traces of an Asiatic origin.

The first European explorers were the Vikings, who sailed to the eastern Arctic about 1000 A.D. However, Martin Frobisher's expeditions in the 1570s were the first recorded visits to the Northwest Territories by an explorer. In 1610, Henry Hudson, while looking for the Northwest Passage, landed briefly on the western shore of the bay that bears his name. His discovery opened the interior of the continent for further exploration.

By the 1700s, the Northwest Territories were dominated by two fur-trading companies: the Hudson's Bay Company based in London, England, and the Northwest Company based in Montreal.

In 1870, the British government transferred control of the North-Western Territory to Canada, and the Hudson's Bay Company sold Rupert's Land for 300,000 pounds sterling. The area was renamed the Northwest Territories. Ten years later the British government annexed the islands of the Arctic archipelago to Canada, which also became part of the Territories.

At some time in their history, the Northwest Territories have included all of Alberta, Saskatchewan, Yukon, and most of Manitoba, Ontario and Quebec.

In 1870, the original tiny province of Manitoba was carved out of the area. In 1905, both Alberta and Saskatchewan were created from the Territories. Manitoba was increased in size in 1880 by taking land from the Territories. In 1898, Yukon became a separate territory. Finally in 1912, the provinces of Manitoba, Ontario and Quebec were enlarged and the Northwest Territories assumed their current boundaries, divided into two districts.

The Northwest Territories remain the largest political subdivision in Canada, with 34.1 percent of the total area of the country.

Date of Entry into Confederation

The Northwest Territories became part of the Dominion of Canada when, in 1870, the British government transferred the North-Western Territory and the Hudson's Bay Company sold Rupert's Land to Canada.

Armorial Bearings

Adopted:
Granted by Queen Elizabeth II on February 24, 1956.

Description:
The white upper third of the shield represents the polar icepack and is crossed by a wavy blue line that symbolizes the Northwest Passage. The lower portion is divided diagonally by a wavy line which represents the treeline; the green stands for the forested areas south of the treeline, and the red represents the tundra to the north.

Minerals and fur, the important bases of northern wealth, are represented by gold billets in the green section and the mask of a white fox in the red. The crest is supported by two narwhals, and the compass rose between them represents the North Pole.

Flag

Adopted:
Ordinance of the Territorial Council assented to January 1, 1969.

Description:
The blue panels at either end of the flag represent the lakes and waters of the Territories. The white centre panel symbolizes the ice and snow of the North, and contains the shield from the arms of the Territories. There was a nationwide competition in 1968 to design the territorial flag; the winner was Robert Bessant of Margaret, Manitoba.

Proportion:
Four by length and two by width. There are three vertical panels; the central one is as wide as the other two combined.

Floral Emblem

Adopted: 1957

Description:
The mountain avens is a member of the rose family, and grows in the Eastern and Central Arctic on high, barren, rocky ground. It has narrow basal leaves, and supports a single white flower on a short stem.

Other Territorial Symbols

Tartan: The Northwest Territories Tartan (registered with the Court of the Lord Lyon, King of Arms of Scotland).

Tree: Jack Pine

Mineral: Native Gold

YUKON

Flag

Coat of Arms

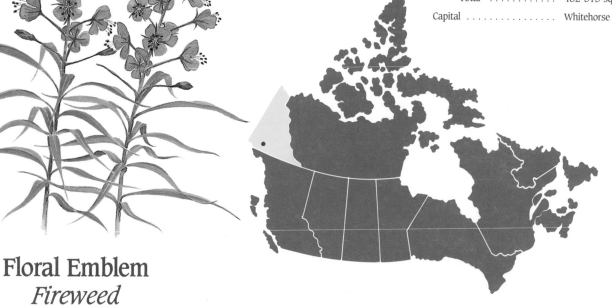

YUKON

Population (1989) 25 400

Area: Land . . . . 478 034 sq km
      Fresh Water . . . .   4 481 sq km
      Total . . . . 482 515 sq km

Capital . . . . Whitehorse

Floral Emblem
Fireweed

Origin of the Name

The name Yukon was first used by the Hudson's Bay Company trader John Bell in 1846. He called it "Yucon," derived from the Loucheaux Indian word "Yuchoo," meaning the big or greatest river. The Yukon River is the fifth largest in North America.

History

Yukon was the first area in Canada to be settled by man. Historians speculate that men and animals once came to North America from Asia across the Bering Strait land bridge. Dialects of Athapaskan, the only Indian language having definite traces of an Asiatic origin, are spoken by the Loucheaux, Han, Tutchone, Kaska-Dena and Tagish Indians. In the south-central part of the territory, the people and language are inland Tlingit, the same as their neighbours and relatives of the coastal Alaskan panhandle.

In 1825, John Franklin became the first European to reach the Yukon when he followed the Arctic shoreline looking for the Northwest Passage. By 1846, the Hudson's Bay Company had established a trading post at Fort Selkirk in central Yukon. However, because of the remote location and the severe climate, the population remained sparse until the discovery of gold.

Between 1897 and 1904, more than $100 million in gold was found in the area surrounding the Klondike River. After the initial discovery at Rabbit Creek (later renamed Bonanza Creek) in 1896, the Klondike became one of the most populous of all regions in northwestern Canada. The city of Dawson was established to accommodate the huge influx of prospectors. There were more than 40,000 people in Dawson at the peak of Klondike fever and it became the new Territory's capital city. In 1898, the *Yukon Act* provided for a Commissioner and an elected legislative assembly, whose size has historically varied on the basis of population.

Once the excitement — and the gold — had disappeared, so did most of the population. Today, Dawson's population is well under 1,000. Whitehorse, which is farther south, is now the Yukon's capital. The population of Yukon today is approximately 25,000.

The Klondike is still a major tourist attraction in Yukon. August 17 is an annual holiday to celebrate the anniversary of the initial discovery of gold at Bonanza Creek.

In 1970, a small Executive Committee was established to assist the Territorial Commissioner in the executive function, and the elected members of the Executive Committee or Council have progressively assumed greater responsibilities. With the introduction of party politics into the general election of the Legislative Assembly in 1978, the Commissioner no longer participates in the Executive Council, and the elected leader of the majority party in the Legislature is the Government Leader. The Government Leader has the authority to determine the size of and the appointments to the Executive Council, paralleling the function of the Premiers and their Cabinets in the provinces.

Date of Entry into Confederation

Present-day Yukon was part of the old North-Western Territory. In 1870, the Dominion of Canada acquired this territory, together with Rupert's Land, and the entire region north of the 60th parallel was known as the Northwest Territories. The boundaries of Yukon were first drawn in 1895, when it became a district of the Northwest Territories. The sudden increase in population during the Klondike gold rush prompted the federal government to give Yukon more control over its affairs. It became a separate territory in 1898 with passage of the *Yukon Act*.

Armorial Bearings

Adopted:
Granted by Queen Elizabeth II on February 24, 1956, and adopted by the Yukon Legislative Council on November 5, 1956.

Description:
The Cross of St. George at the top of the shield refers to the early explorers and fur traders from England, and the roundel of heraldic fur in the centre of the cross symbolizes the fur trade. The wavy white and blue vertical stripes in the lower part represent the Yukon River and the rivers and creeks where gold was discovered. The red spire-like forms represent the mountains of Yukon, and two gold discs in each spire symbolize the Territory's mineral resources. The crest is a malamute dog standing on a mound of snow. The dog played an important role in the early history of Yukon and is noted for its loyalty, stamina and strength.

Flag

Adopted:
Ordinance of the Territorial Council assented to December 1, 1967

Description:
The flag consists of three vertical panels. The green panel on the staff side symbolizes the green taiga forests, the white in the centre, the winter snows, and the blue on the fly represents the deep blue of the northern waters. The centre panel also features the floral emblem, the fireweed, and the Arms of Yukon. The flag was designed by Lynn Lambert, a Haines Junction student, who won the flag-designing competition during Canada's centennial year.

Proportion:
The flag is two by length and one by width. The centre vertical panel is one and a half times the width of the other two.

Floral Emblem

Adopted: November 16, 1957

Description:
The fireweed is a pale purple flower that grows in abundance throughout the territory and blooms during June, July and August. The hardy fireweed is so named because it is usually the first flower to appear in burned-over areas.

Other Territorial Symbols

Tartan: The Yukon Tartan
Gemstone: Lazulite
Bird: The Common Raven

Suggestions for Classroom Activities

These seven activity pages have been designed to assist teachers in developing classroom programmes based on the theme of Canadian citizenship. Teachers are urged to take an integrated approach to the teaching of this study unit, taking advantage of possible learning experiences in all areas of the curriculum.

Teachers are encouraged to have the activity pages colour photocopied and distributed to the students to foster classroom participation. The following teaching ideas are intended to be starting points for classroom activities. Teachers will want to adapt and modify these and other learning experiences to meet the needs of their particular class.

There are an endless number of possibilities for student participation, based on the material in this booklet. For example, a quiz could be developed using information extracted from the text on the national, provincial and territorial pages. A possibility for more active student involvement would be to have the class participate in historical, role playing. Some students could be assigned to represent provinces or territories already in Confederation while others would represent British North American colonies that are contemplating union with Canada. The resulting debate could lead to a greater understanding of our historical past as well as an appreciation of our evolution into nationhood and what it means to be a Canadian citizen.

ABCDEFGHIJKLMNOPQRSTUVWXYZ

1 GETTING STARTED

Use the *Symbols Around Us* page to draw students' attention to everyday symbols that they encounter. Have students begin a symbol search using the newspaper, yellow pages, school, home, community and other sources that could spark a sense of adventure.

Present the enclosed Dominion of Canada poster to your class. Discuss the various Canadian symbols, pictorial representations and other material contained on both the national and provincial/territorial sides.

2 CANADIAN FLAGS

Use the *Canadian Flags* page to identify the flags shown and discuss the story that each one tells.

Have students note where they see flags flying in their community. Assign students different provinces and territories and ask them to write an imaginative story of a young boy or girl in that area of the country.

3 COATS OF ARMS

Discuss the meaning of the coats of arms presented on the *Armorial Bearings* page. Translate Canada's motto (*A Mari usque ad Mare*) into as many languages as possible.

Have students use the *Personal Coat of Arms* page to tap their creativity in drawing a personal coat of arms containing their favourite and most important belongings.

4 EMBLEMS OF CANADA

Ask students to list where they see the beaver and maple leaf used as symbols during a one-week period. Have students draw maple leaves in various colours and make a collage.

5 FLORAL EMBLEMS

Use the *Floral Emblem* page to identify the floral emblems shown and to discuss the location and characteristics of each one.

Research the wildflowers growing near your school or at a local conservation area.

Create giant tissue paper imitations of the provincial and territorial flowers for a *'Canada Bouquet'* in the school foyer or gym.

6 STAMPS OF CANADA

Use the *Stamps of Canada* page as a springboard for the study of Canadian stamps.

Student stamp collectors might enjoy presenting their collections to the class.

7 CANADIAN COINAGE

Using the *Canadian Coinage* page, assign students a different coin and ask them to explain what each pictorial representation means to them. Two teams of students could be assigned voyages on the *Bluenose* dime. Have each team tell their story of a 'week's voyage.'

8 SUPPLEMENTING ACTIVITIES

Encourage students to write a *What Canada Means to Me* essay and to investigate the schedule of events planned for upcoming holiday celebrations in their community. Write out the words to *O Canada* and *God Save the Queen* and have your students copy them down to foster memorization and a discussion of their meaning.

A year-end Canada Day assembly could involve displays of student work and class projects, choral readings, a guest speaker (local politician), Canadian folk songs, a Canada Cake prepared by students, slides brought in by students from trips taken to different parts of Canada, and special Canada Day messages.

Symbols around us

We see symbols all around us every day. Symbols communicate a message to us in picture form. Symbols are used to identify companies, teams, rules, stores, products and many, many more things.

1. Can you identify each symbol below?

2. Where have you seen each one?

3. Why is each one so important to us?

4. Make a list of some other symbols you have seen. Compare lists with your friends and discuss them.

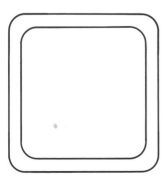

Make up a symbol that you think should be used and explain why.

Canadian flags

Every province and territory in Canada has its own flag. However, the one symbol that unites us all is the red and white national flag of Canada, first raised on February 15, 1965.

1. Label each flag below with the name of the province or territory to which it belongs.

2. Study the flags carefully. Do you see any features that are the same?

3. What story does each flag tell?

4. Make a list of all the different places in your community where the Canadian flag is being flown.

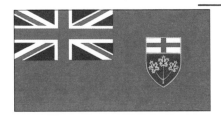

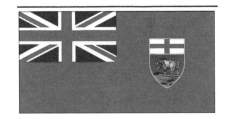
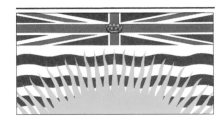

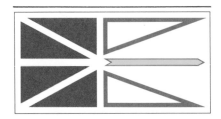

Armorial bearings

Coats of arms first appeared during the Middle Ages when they were painted on shields and banners to identify knights fighting in battles and tournaments. Today, countries have coats of arms which help identify them and help tell the story of their past.

1. Write the name of the Canadian province or territory to which each shield below belongs.

2. Study the shields carefully. Do you see any features that are the same?

3. What story does each shield tell?

4. The Canadian coat of arms is the only symbol that appears on every denomination of Canadian paper money. Look around. Can you find the coat of arms anywhere else?

Personal coat of arms

Coats of arms are symbols used to identify and represent royalty, countries, cities, hospitals, universities, individuals, private companies, and other corporate bodies. Coats of arms help to "tell the story" of the people they represent.

1. Create your own personal coat of arms by completing each section of the shield below.

2. When you are finished, share your coat of arms with a friend.

3. Now that you have made a coat of arms for yourself, you might like to design one for your class or school. Put it up for others to see.

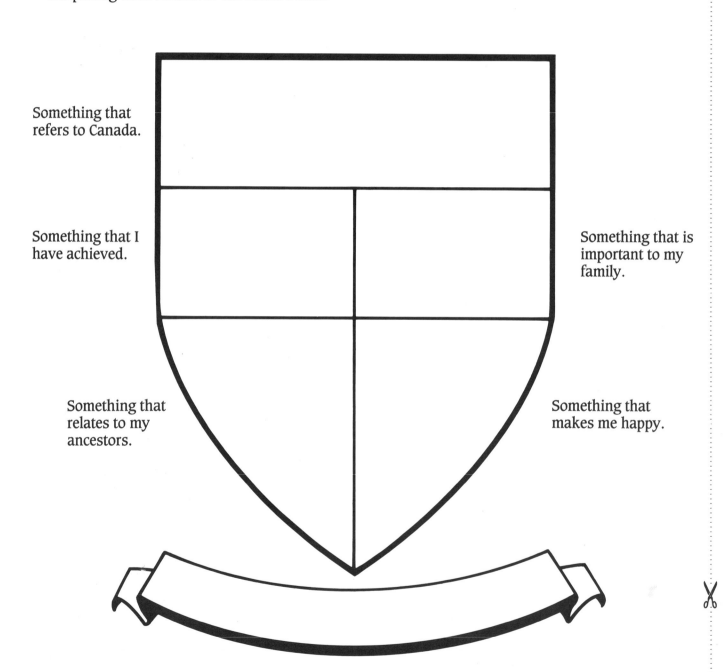

Something that refers to Canada.

Something that I have achieved.

Something that is important to my family.

Something that relates to my ancestors.

Something that makes me happy.

Make up a personal motto.

Floral emblems

Each province and territory has adopted a special flower that serves as a symbol of that part of Canada. The floral emblem of each province and territory is listed below.

2. Canada does not have a national floral emblem. If you could pick one flower to represent our country, which one would it be? Why?

3. Of all the flowers you know, which one would you choose as your own floral emblem? Why?

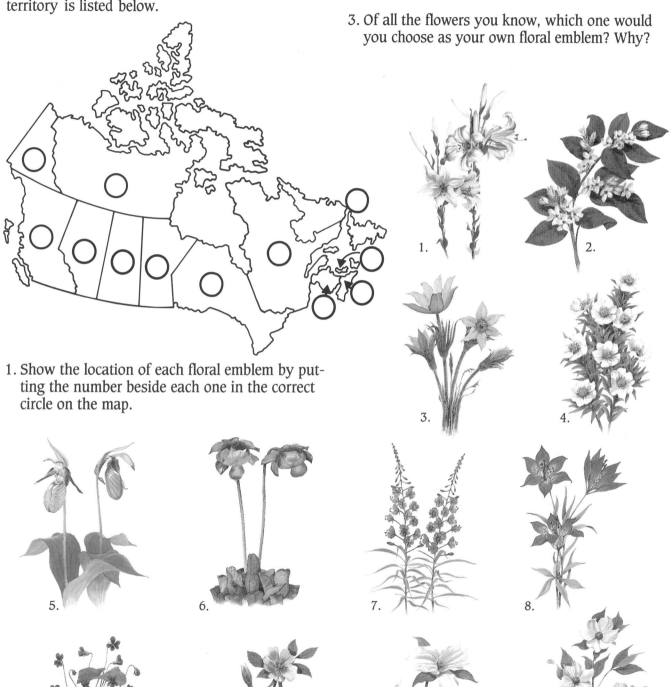

1. Show the location of each floral emblem by putting the number beside each one in the correct circle on the map.

1.

2.

3.

4.

5.

6.

7.

8.

9.

10.

11.

12.

Stamps of Canada

Stamp collecting is an excellent way to learn about people and happenings all over the world. You can discover a great deal about Canada by studying the words, pictures and symbols on its postage stamps. Stamps help to tell Canada's story.

Her Majesty
Queen Elizabeth II

The National Flag
of Canada

1. What is the predominant symbol on this stamp?

2. What does VR stand for? What does this tell you about the age of the stamp?

The 50¢ Bluenose stamp was issued on January 6, 1929. The Bluenose was built in Nova Scotia, and has been called the greatest racing schooner of all time.

1. The Bluenose is the Canadian symbol that appears on one of our coins. Which one?

2. Can you spot another Canadian symbol in the top corners of this stamp?

1. What police force is shown on this stamp?

2. Make up a story about an average day for the Mountie and his horse.

Create your own Canadian stamp in this space. You might like to use Canadian symbols in your design, or you could put your own ideas to work.

Canadian coinage

Canada did not have its own coins until the mid-1800s. Prior to this, coins from France, Great Britain, Spain, Spanish America, Portugal, and the United States were used.

1. Name each coin. What symbol appears on each?

2. How much would you have if you had one of each coin?

3. Whose picture is on the front of each coin? Why?

Think of a new design for a Canadian coin. Share your design with a friend.

WHERE TO WRITE FOR ADDITIONAL INFORMATION

Information on the Crown in Canada and poster size photographs of Her Majesty The Queen and His Excellency the Governor General, suitable for framing, are available from:

Information Services Directorate
Government House
1 Sussex Drive
Ottawa, Ontario
K1A 0A1
(613) 991-2249

Ontario Travel
Queen's Park
Toronto, Ontario
M7A 2E5
Tel: (416) 965-3448
or English: 1-800-268-3755 (except Yukon & N.W.T.)
French: 1-800-268-3736

Communication-Québec Branch
1500C Charest Blvd. West, 1st floor
Ste-Foy, Québec
G1N 2E5
Tel: (418) 643-1430

Supervisor of Public Inquiries
Nova Scotia Information Service
P.O. Box 608
Halifax, Nova Scotia
B3J 2R7
Tel: (902) 424-5200

New Brunswick Inquiries
P.O. Box 6000
Fredericton, New Brunswick
E3B 5H1
Toll free: 1-800-442-4400

Travel Manitoba
7th floor — 155 Carlton Street
Winnipeg, Manitoba
R3C 3H8
Tel: (204) 945-3777
Toll free: 1-800-665-0040

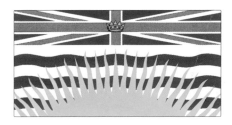

Tourguides
Ministry of Tourism
and Provincial Secretary
Government of British Columbia
Victoria, British Columbia
V8V 1X4
Tel: (604) 387-3046

Information on matters pertaining to heraldry is available from the Chief Herald of Canada:

Since 1868, the Department of the Secretary of State of Canada has held responsibility for promoting understanding and awareness of Canada's national symbols and for organizing state ceremonies. The Department gives advice, assistance and information on such matters to provincial and territorial governments, institutions and organizations as well as the general public. For further information, please contact:

The Canadian Heraldic Authority
Government House
1 Sussex Drive
Ottawa, Ontario
K1A 0A1
(613) 991-2230

State Ceremonial Branch
Department of the Secretary of State of Canada
Ottawa, Ontario
K1A 0M5
(819) 994-1616

Island Information Service
P.O. Box 2000
Charlottetown, Prince Edward Island
C1A 7N8
Tel: (902) 368-4000

Visual Identity Office
Saskatchewan Property Management
Corporation
2045 Broad Street
Regina, Saskatchewan
S4P 3V7
Tel: (306) 787-6520

Department of Tourism
15th floor
10025 Jasper Avenue
Edmonton, Alberta
T5J 3Z3
Tel: (403) 427-4321
Toll free: 1-800-661-8888

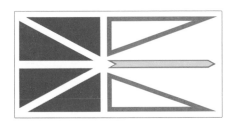

Department of Development & Tourism
Tourism Branch
P.O. Box 2016
St. John's, Newfoundland
A1C 5R8
Tel: (709) 576-2830

Department of Culture & Communications
Government of Northwest Territories
P.O. Box 1320
Yellowknife, N.W.T.
X1A 2L9
Tel: (403) 873-7442

The Inquiry Centre
Executive Council Office
Government of Yukon
P.O. Box 2703
Whitehorse, Yukon
Y1A 2C6
Tel: (403) 667-5811 or 667-5812